THE NEW YORK

Yankees

THE NEW YORK

Yankees

Legendary Heroes, Magical Moments, and Amazing Statistics Through the Decades

Jay David

William Morrow and Company, Inc.

New York

Batting and pitching summaries excerpted with permission of Macmillan USA, a Simon & Schuster Macmillan Company, from THE BASEBALL EN-CYCLOPEDIA, Ninth Edn. Copyright © 1993 by Macmillan Publishing Company.

It is the policy of William Morrow and Company, Inc., and its imprints and affiliates, recognizing the importance of preserving what has been written, to print the books we publish on acid-free paper, and we exert our best efforts to that end.

Library of Congress Cataloging-in-Publication Data

Adler, Bill.
    The New York Yankees : legendary heroes, magical moments, and amaz-ing statistics through the decades / Jay David.
      p. cm.
    ISBN 0-688-15505-7
    1. New York Yankees (Baseball team)—History. I. Title.
    GV875.N4A35 1997
    796.357′64′097471—dc21   97-1326
                                                  CIP

Printed in the United States of America

First Edition

1 2 3 4 5 6 7 8 9 10

BOOK DESIGN BY LEAH S. CARLSON

Contents

YANKEES FANS CELEBRATE THE 1996 WORLD SERIES VICTORY WITH AN OLD-FASHIONED
TICKERTAPE PARADE. ANDREA RENAULT/GLOBE PHOTOS, INC.

Introduction

No great baseball team is born overnight. What made the 1996 Yankees world champions was the tradition, now nearly a century long, of great players: Babe Ruth, Lou Gehrig, Joe DiMaggio, Whitey Ford, Mickey Mantle, Roger Maris, Reggie Jackson, Don Mattingly, and dozens of others. The games they played, the legendary home runs and no-hitters, the MVPs, and Hall of Famers, the exhilarating highs and devastating lows—all are brought to life again in this special tribute to the New York Yankees: 1903–1996.

The Early
Years

THE NEW YORK YANKEE TEAM WAS BORN IN 1903. ACTUALLY IT WAS THE transported remnants of the original Baltimore Orioles of the National League (the Orioles of today started in 1954 when the St. Louis Browns went to Baltimore), which had been declared an American League team and sent to New York to compete with the New York Giants. The club was first called the Highlanders, sometimes the Hilltoppers, because their ballpark, Hilltop Park in upper Manhattan was on such high ground.

The press liked the name "Yankees" better, and around 1908 began popularizing it—for one reason, it was less cumbersome for print than Highlanders. And the players also preferred "Yankees." But it was not until 1913 that it became the official name of the club.

THE YANKS' EARLY BALL FIELDS WERE A FAR CRY FROM TODAY'S STADIUM. MARDIE HOLTON, GLOVE PHOTOS, INC.

In 1903 the Yankees, the new team of the new American League, were deep in the shadows of the two New York National League teams, the New York Giants and the Brooklyn Dodgers.

And they were fated to stay there for a number of years. The Giants at the Polo Grounds were *the* New York team. And Brooklyn loved the Brooklyn Dodgers. But the new American League had solid backing, and the interloping Yankees were here to stay. Three teams in New York provided good competition for loyalty from the fans.

Byron "Ban" Johnson, the president of the American League, who loathed New York Giants manager John J. McGraw and wanted nothing more than to see him bested by the Yanks, prevailed upon two adventurous and imaginative New Yorkers, Frank Farrell and Bill Devery, to ante up $18,000 to buy the fledgling ball club.

Devery and Farrell were quite a pair—Devery was a onetime police officer of suspect ethics; Farrell owned a racing stable and ran a saloon and gambling houses. Farrell had plenty of money, and his checkered past bothered many of his associates, but nobody had the guts to challenge him.

To make the team a bit more attractive to Devery and Farrell, Johnson added some star players. Among his most notable contributions were outfielder Wee

Willie Keeler from Brooklyn and Happy Jack Chesbro, a pitcher from the Pittsburgh Pirates. (Both were inducted into the Baseball Hall of Fame, Keeler in 1939 and Chesbro in 1946, the first Yankee pitcher to have that honor.)

Chesbro's achievements were considerable. He won 21 games at least five times in his major league career and four times in a row. Unfortunately, his aim wasn't always perfect—his pitches hit a lifetime total of 109 batters, making him fourteenth in the all-time list.

Chesbro worked hard. He was third on an all-time Yankee complete-game list (169) and ninth on their all-time innings-pitched list (1,953). That was even more impressive because he ranked tenth on the Yanks' win list (128), games started (227), and strikeouts (913).

He started and lost the first game in Yankee history, bowing to the Washington Senators on April 22, 1903; but in the team's first home opener, April 30, 1903, he defeated the Senators, 6–2. He won 41 games in 1904, his best year, earning an American League record that could stand for all time.

But even with such a superstar on the team, the Yankees could not seem to win pennants. In fact, Chesbro in 1904 blew a ninth-inning pitch the last day of the season, allowing Boston to score the game's winning run to capture the American League pennant. So, understandably, in 1905 Yankee fan attendance plummeted, taking a dive of 30 percent from 1904. Then in their thirties, both Chesbro and right fielder Willie Keeler were losing their allure with the younger fans. And to boot, just down the road at the Polo Grounds, the Giants capped their 1905 season by winning the World Series.

As the seasons progressed, and the Yankees did not perform up to decent standards, Devery and Farrell became more contentious, both with each other and the team staff—*and* with the players as well. When, in 1910, the Yankee manager George Stallings accused a star player, a great first baseman Hal Chase, of throwing games, Farrell was absolutely incensed; Stallings left and Farrell appointed Chase manager.

Incidentally, Chase was a gambler himself, and couldn't seem to avoid getting into trouble wherever he went. And though he was a great draw for fans, creating big attendance records, he was involved in several altercations with the brass during his stay with the Yankees.

In 1913, sportswriter Heywood Broun wrote a piece accusing Chase of throwing games. Farrell raised Cain with Broun about his column. But then, in a complete reversal of tactics, he traded Chase to the White Sox just a few days after the column appeared.

In spite of the fact that the Yankees couldn't win any pennants or World Series for Devery and Farrell, the team with its stars managed some astonishing stats. For example, in 1906, the team successfully sacrificed 178 times—a club record that stands to this very day. They also put together a winning streak of 15 games, which has been exceeded only three times.

And from August 30 to September 4, the Yankees won both ends of 5 consecutive doubleheaders.

In 1914, there was another amazing feat: In the game played on August 3, the catcher, Les Nunamaker, cut down three runners attempting to steal bases *in one inning*. This defensive play reflected the team's yearly defense measures, bringing them in with a solid finishing record (.963).

In April 1911 a fire burned down the Polo Grounds. In an unusual move, Frank Farrell offered to share Hilltop Park with the Giants for the rest of the season, and the Giants accepted gratefully. That year the Yankees managed to break even, but in 1912 they wound up in the cellar with a 50–102 record.

Although 1913 was the year the Yankees had a lasting real name of their own, their ten-year lease at Hilltop Park was up and they asked the Giants if they could share the newly rebuilt Polo Grounds, renting their space and paying for their expenses. The Giants agreed. At the Polo Grounds the Yanks found they had more fans than they had had at Hilltop Park. But that year, in which Hal Chase was dealt out to the White Sox, there was little difference in their performance from the year before. At the helm for a while was

Frank Chance of the Tinker-to-Evers-to-Chance double play. He, however, didn't get along with either the owners or Chase and left before season's end.

In 1914 the Yanks tied for sixth place, not much better. By 1915 change was in the air—and change occurred. Devery and Farrell were disgusted with the drain on their resources, and frustrated at their inability to get the team going so it could win a few pennants or at least look good in the ratings. But they could hardly complain about the money they made when they sold the Yankees in 1915. Having paid a paltry $18,000 for the club, they sold it for $460,000.

The new owners were Col. Jacob Ruppert and Tillingast L'Hommedieu Huston, who became a colonel in World War I. Ruppert was a colonel in the 7th Regiment of the National Guard. Huston had been a captain in the Spanish-American War and he was always called Cap by those close to him.

Huston was a big, affable, jovial man with a great appetite and a big man's taste for good beer. He let little pass him by, enjoying things in a picturesque and colorful fashion. When he and Ruppert signed the contract for the Yankees, he amazed everyone present by reaching into his pocket and pulling out a wad of money big enough to choke a horse—230 thousand-dollar bills.

If Colonel Ruppert, a sportsman, was less flamboyant than Huston he was much more astute at finances and much more aware of how to run a business—particularly a million-dollar business—which the Yankees soon became. Ruppert's grandfather, having emigrated from Bavaria, founded the Ruppert brewery (Knickerbocker beer) in New York in 1851. His son took over the business in 1867, the same year Jacob Ruppert was born.

Young Ruppert immediately entered into the spirit of the family business and learned it from top to bottom. No fool, he was a determined and intelligent man. Management of all kinds fascinated him. Not an innovator, he was if anything someone who perfected what was already "in place." Not for nothing was he to be called—and correctly—the "Master Builder in Baseball."

Ruppert, probably more than Houston, was aware of what they had purchased in the New York Yankees: an enfranchisement that needed repair badly. He once said that he had purchased "an orphan ball club, without a home of its own, without players of outstanding ability, without prestige."

Although they immediately hired a new manager and some players, both Ruppert and Huston kept their eyes open for good new players who would help the languishing franchise. And even more for a manager who would turn the tide. Enter Miller Huggins, who became the first of the great Yankee managers. After five years with St. Louis managing the Cardinals, a respected and famed figure before he ever donned pinstripes, Huggins was the manager recommended to Ruppert by Ban Johnson.

Miller Huggins had more nicknames than most guys in baseball did: "Little Mr. Everywhere," "Mighty Mite," and "Rabbit," because he was tiny, wiry, and fast. "The Lawyer" because he'd studied law before baseball, and "Hug" just because.

He was a dynamite player before turning to managing, hitting better than .300 a season at St. Paul (1901–03). In 1904 he joined the Cincinnati Reds playing second base until 1909. He was the first to perfect what came to be called the "delayed steal"—and he was good at it. Batting, he crouched at the plate, shrinking his strike zone, drawing many walks. He played for St. Louis (1910–16), becoming a player-manager in 1913.

MILLER HUGGINS
AP/WIDE WORLD

Commenting on going unnoticed because of his size: "[John J.] McGraw and I could enter a crowded room at the same time and be introduced—and in two minutes the crowd would be all around McGraw and nobody would even remember I was there."

Huggins's appearance in New York in 1918 became an immediate source of irreparable contention between Ruppert and Huston. Huston had his own candidate, who was a friend—Wilbert Robinson, a very popular and rotund character (5′8½″, 215 pounds) who had in 1917 completed his fourth of eighteen seasons with the Brooklyn Dodgers. Ruppert disagreed: He wasn't impressed with Robinson, who in his fifties, he thought was too old. Not that Ruppert was that enthusiastic about Huggins either. Huggins's blue-collar bearing and appearance—plus the fact he was a shrimp of a man at 5′6½″, and 140 pounds—went against Ruppert's grain.

Huston at the time was in uniform in France, fighting a war against the kaiser in Germany; in his absence, Ruppert, convinced of Huggins's prowess by Johnson and Huggins himself, brought Huggins aboard. Huston, from Europe, objected roundly.

Miller's stay with the Yankees was one of conflict as well as triumph. He was plunged into the midst of a losing team, involved in constant in-fighting among its members, to turn it around. But Miller was no pussycat. Though small and roosterlike, he had his own surly and sometimes ugly manner. It

Q: When was the spitball declared illegal?

A: 1920.

was bound to be an eventful stay. And so the be-
leaguered Yankees drifted into the decade of the
1920s. . . .

JACK CHESBRO

Yr.	Team	W	L	PCT	ERA	G	GS	CG	IP	H	BB	SO
1899	PIT N	6	9	.400	4.11	19	17	15	149	165	59	28
1900		15	13	.536	3.67	32	26	20	215.2	220	79	56
1901		21	10	.677	2.38	36	28	26	287.2	261	52	129
1902		28	6	.824	2.17	35	33	31	286.1	242	62	136
1903	NY A	21	15	.583	2.77	40	36	33	324.2	300	74	147
1904		41	12	.774	1.82	55	51	48	454.2	338	88	239
1905		19	15	.559	2.20	41	38	24	303.1	262	71	156
1906		24	16	.600	2.96	49	42	24	325	314	75	152
1907		10	10	.500	2.53	30	25	17	206	192	46	78
1908		14	20	.412	2.93	45	31	21	289	271	67	124
1909	2 teams	NY	A	(9G 0–4)		BOS	A	(1G 0–1)				
"	total	0	5	.000	6.14	10	5	2	55.2	77	17	20
11 yrs.		199	131	.603	2.68	392	332	261	2897	2642	690	1265

BABE RUTH PUT THE YANKEES ON THE MAP. NBC/GLOBE PHOTOS, INC.

The Roaring
Twenties

THE YANKEES REMAINED THE POOR
RELATIVES ON THE NEW YORK
baseball scene as the roaring twenties
approached. The Giants had been
present since 1883, winning pennants in 1904 and 1905, the World
Series in 1905, and more pennants in 1911,
1912, and 1913. The Dodgers had won pen-

nants in 1899, 1900, 1916, and 1920.

Ruppert wanted to win and he thought he had an answer.

The Babe.

Babe Ruth had made the Boston Red Sox big winners in the six seasons he had been with them. He had won 89 games, pitching—those were Boston's greatest years, with Ruth as their greatest player. During his stint with the Red Sox, they won the World Series four times. In 1919 Ruth had hit an amazing total of 29 home runs. He was *something.*

Ruppert had grown confident that feisty Miller Huggins was the right manager. Could he mold a winning team around the Babe, that is, if they could get him?

All it took was money, which Jake Ruppert had. Harry Frazee, the owner of the Red Sox, was short on cash and had baseball and theatrical debts. He also wanted to keep financing Broadway shows. Ruppert played on that and cajoled Frazee into selling the Bambino to the Yankees. Ruppert got Ruth for $125,000 in cash and a loan to Frazee of $350,000 with a mortgage on Fenway Park.

Babe Ruth had come to Boston from Baltimore, where he was born on the waterfront on February 6, 1895. His full name was George Herman Ruth, Jr. He was the oldest child of a barkeep and his wife. His mother had seven children after George Herman, but only one of them, a sister, lived past infancy.

"I think my mother hated me," Ruth once confided to a friend. He believed that both parents blamed him for the deaths of his brothers and sisters. Perhaps they did. Whatever he was, he was a handful for his mother and his father. When he was seven years old his mother and father wrote him

off as "incorrigible" and sent him to St. Mary's Industrial Home for Boys, an orphanage/reformatory, where he learned how to play baseball. Then, at the age of nineteen, he was out of there—to play baseball.

January 5, 1920, the day that the signatures were applied to the contract between the Red Sox and the Yankees to ship Babe Ruth down to the Yankees in New York, marked the beginning of the Roaring Twenties. It was also the beginning of the era in which—thanks in great part to Jake Ruppert's money and in even greater part to his knowledge of how to pull a ball team together to make it a winner—the Yankees became the elite and prestigious team they were for much of the twentieth century.

It all had to do with the Babe. In his Yankee career he outdid himself. His 29 home runs in his last year in Boston were soon eclipsed. In 1920 he hit 54 home runs for New York, batted in 171 runs, and caused 177 runs to be scored. In 1921, he led both the American and National Leagues in home runs—knocking in 59, with 457 total bases.

Q. Why did the Yankee uniform have pinstripes?

A. Jacob Ruppert, who designed the team's new pin-striped uniform in 1923, thought the stripes would make Babe Ruth look slimmer.

Sportswriters vied with one another to invent new nicknames for him. One of the first had Italian origins—the "Bambino" (the "Babe"). It fit. Others were the "Behemoth of Bust," the "Rajah of Rap," the "Caliph of Clout," the "Maharajah of Mash," the "Wazir of Wham," and, of course, the "Sultan of Swat." His teammates simply called him "Jidge" or "Jidgie"— short for "George"—and he called most of them "Keed," since he could never remember their names.

And his stats kept on growing and growing. In 1923 the Sultan of Swat hit 41 homers, and 46 in 1924. Ruth had initiated what can be called the long-ball game, a game of big homers, and he was the home run king. In the Yankees' great year of 1927, the Babe set his own record for home runs—60 in one season.

In 1928 he almost equaled that record, hitting 54. Though he was slacking off just a mite, the Yankees weren't. What had started with Ruth followed with others. In the 1920s in large part due to Ruppert's wherewithal and the baseball acumen of business manager Ed Barrow (elected to the Hall of Fame in 1953) the Yankees built up a powerhouse.

Earlier in the decade the trouble that had been simmering between the two Yankee owners throughout the years, beginning with Huston's anger at Ruppert's selection of Huggins as manager, finally came to a head. In May 1923 Ruppert finally got Huston to agree to sell his half of the Yankees to him for $1,500,000. Huston "took the money and ran."

Though the partnership was dead, the Yankees were very much alive and thriving. The addition of Ruth immediately propelled the Yankees into the World Series—which had been forbidden territory up to 1921. They played in but lost the World Series in 1921 and 1922 to the Giants, but beat them in a 6-game Series in 1923. They were blanked out in 1924 and 1925, and then lost the Series in 1926 to the St. Louis Cardinals. They won the Series both in 1927

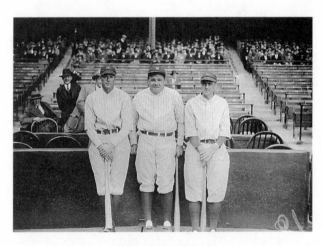

THREE ON MURDERERS' ROW:
BOB MEUSEL, BABE RUTH, AND EARLE COMBS
AP/WIDE WORLD

against Pittsburgh and in 1928 against St. Louis in an awesome display of pitching and hitting—4–0 each year. They didn't make the Series at all in 1929.

The 1927 lineup, in many people's eyes probably the greatest baseball team ever fielded, was known as "Murderers' Row." In that lineup were right fielder Babe Ruth, center fielder Earle Combs, third baseman Bob Meusel, second baseman Tony Lazzeri, and first baseman Lou Gehrig.

• "Sixty . . . count 'em." •

On September 30, 1927, in the Yankees final game with the Washington Senators, Babe Ruth hit his famous sixtieth homer of the season, facing Tom Zachary on the mound. This is *The New York Times*'s record of that formidable blow: "The first Zachary offering was a fast one which sailed over for a called strike. The next was high. The Babe took a vicious swing at the third pitched ball and the bat connected with a crash that was audible in all parts of the stand. It was not necessary to follow the course of the ball. The boys in the bleachers indicated the route of the record homer. It dropped about halfway to the top." The Babe jogged around the bases, touching each bag firmly and carefully. When he spiked the rubber at home plate to record homer number 60, there were screams all over the stadium and hats were tossed into the air, papers shredded, and thrown everywhere. In the locker room at the end of the game, Ruth could hardly contain himself. "Sixty, count 'em! Sixty!" he shouted. "Let's see some other son of a bitch match that!"

The two, Ruth and Gehrig, with the Babe batting first and Gehrig following him, formed a double whammy that was formidable to opposing pitchers. Gehrig was as dangerous as Ruth—in fact, Jimmie Fox once said he was "more dangerous" than Ruth. The sight of Gehrig on deck was quite enough to take the steam out of some of the pitches to Ruth. It was a psychological zap, giving the advantage to the Bambino.

They were twin threats, both with astonishing batting averages. But there any similarity between the two ended. Ruth had already become a national hero by the time that Gehrig joined the Yankees in 1923, and he overshadowed him in publicity and acclaim. Gehrig was a different type of person from Ruth, a modest person content to stay out of the spotlight. While Ruth threw his money around and spent most of his nights on the town, Gehrig was very thrifty with his cash and rarely was seen visiting the various haunts in the many cities they played in.

Ruth, a bit rough around the edges, was a hell-raiser. Gehrig was by instinct and bearing a polished gentleman. He was proud of his pinstripes and would do nothing to tarnish the image of a Yankee ballplayer. Because of the different personalities of the two men, Ruth attracted much publicity and Gehrig shunned it, even avoiding being quoted in print. "I'm not a head-line guy," he once said.

Lou Gehrig grew up in New York City, the son of immigrant parents who had come to the United States from Germany in 1900. He became a baseball star at Commerce High in Manhattan. Having won the New York City championship, Commerce beat Lane Tech, the Chicago champs, at Wrigley Field, 12–6, thanks to

LOU GEHRIG. GLOBE PHOTOS, INC.

a grand slam homer of Lou Gehrig's. The New York *Daily News* called Gehrig "the New York lad known as the 'Babe Ruth' of the high schools."

At Columbia University Gehrig played both baseball and football. John J. Mc-Graw, the New York Giants manager, sent Gehrig to the Hartford minor league club, having him play under an assumed name while still going to Columbia. The ruse was discovered and Gehrig was humiliated. He never really forgave McGraw for talking him into that kind of deceit.

In June 1923 Gehrig was signed up by the Yankees. He played for Hartford of the Eastern League, with which the Yanks were working, then finished each season with the Yanks. On September 27, 1923, as a Yankee player, he hit his first major league home run

WAITE HOYTE, HALL OF FAMER WHO PLAYED WITH THE YANKEES IN THE 1927 WORLD SERIES: "THE ONE INTANGIBLE FACTOR WAS THEIR UTTER BELIEF IN THEIR INVINCIBILITY. IT TRANSCENDED THAT WORTHWHILE BUT RATHER OVERWORKED TERM, 'SPIRIT'—IT WASN'T THE DASH, THE VERVE, THE HIP-HIP, LET'S GO GET 'EM STUFF. . . . YOU HAD TO EXPERIENCE THE YEAR TO BELIEVE WHAT YOU SAW. THERE WAS THE POSITIVE CONFIDENCE THAT NO TEAM COULD BEAT THEM—FREAKISH IN ITS NATURE, ABETTED BY THE SUPER-SUPER PERFOR-MANCES OF RUTH, GEHRIG, LAZZERI, DUGAN, COMBS, MEUSEL, AND THE OTHERS."

in Boston's Fenway Park. In 1923–24, he had 38 at bats for 17 hits, driving in 15 runs. He was made a permanent Yankee in 1925.

He warmed the bench that year until June 1, when he pinch-hit for Pee Wee Wanniger. The next day Wally Pipp, the regular first baseman, was unable to play. The Iron Horse was sent out to play first base— and he stayed in the Yankee lineup for fourteen years.

His stats kept improving. The year 1927 was a banner year for him, as well as for the rest of the Yankees. He was named Most Valuable Player of the American League. He hit 52 doubles, setting the Yankee club record until 1986 when Don Mattingly hit 53. He made 117 extra-base hits that year. He combined with Ruth for 107 home runs, the most ever hit by two players in one club—up to Roger Maris and Mickey Mantle in 1961 with 115. Gehrig had 175 RBIs despite the fact that Ruth, who batted ahead of him, cleared the bases 60 times, leaving him with no one to bat in.

Lou Gehrig held the career record for most consecutive games played—2,130—until September 6, 1995, the day (night) Cal Ripken of the Baltimore Orioles played in his 2,131 consecutive game against the California Angels.

· The House That Ruth Built ·

By 1920, it was obvious that the Yankees and the Giants needed something bigger than the Polo Gounds to play in. Eventually Charlie Stoneham, the owner of the Giants, gave the ultimatum: the Yankees had to leave. Mc-Graw, the Giants manager, agreed. "Chase the Yankees out of the Polo Grounds and make them build their own park in the Bronx, because once they go up there, they will be forgotten."

Ruppert and Huston bought 11.6 acres in the Bronx and built a stadium, completed in April 1923, and only six-

FROM 1923 TO 1973, THE OLD YANKEES STADIUM IN THE BRONX STOOD AS A TRIBUTE TO BABE RUTH'S BATTING TALENTS. GLOBE PHOTOS, INC.

teen minutes by subway from Forty-second Street. The playing field was asymmetrical, with two bulges in the center and in left field. It was 281 feet down the left-field line, 295 feet down the right-field line, and 490 feet to dead center. It was built for pull hitters, not for straight-on power hitters. The key dimension—orchestrated in favor of Babe Ruth's left-handed batting prowess—was the relatively short distance in right field. In the House That Ruth Built, on Opening Day, April 18, 1923, the Bambino hit a mighty homer in the bottom of the third against Boston, and the Yanks took it, 4–1, to a full crowd. Once Yankee Stadium stood, the Yankees outdrew the Giants. "Yankee Stadium was a mistake," Jake Ruppert once said, "not mine, but the Giants'."

LOU GEHRIG

Yr.	Team	G	BA	SA	AB	H	2B	3B	HR	R	RBI	BB	SB
1923	NY A	13	.423	.769	26	11	4	1	1	6	9	2	0
1924		10	.500	.583	12	6	1	0	0	2	5	1	0
1925		126	.295	.531	437	129	23	10	20	73	68	46	6
1926		155	.313	.549	572	179	47	20	16	135	107	105	6
1927		155	.373	.765	584	218	52	18	47	149	175	109	10
1928		154	.374	.648	562	210	47	13	27	139	142	95	4
1929		154	.300	.582	553	166	33	9	35	127	126	122	4
1930		154	.379	.721	581	220	42	17	41	143	174	101	12
1931		155	.341	.662	619	211	31	15	46	163	184	117	17
1932		156	.349	.621	596	208	42	9	34	138	151	108	4
1933		152	.334	.605	593	198	41	12	32	138	139	92	9
1934		154	.363	.706	579	210	40	6	49	128	165	109	9
1935		149	.329	.583	535	176	26	10	30	125	119	132	8
1936		155	.354	.696	579	205	37	7	49	167	152	130	3
1937		157	.351	.643	569	200	37	9	37	138	159	127	4
1938		157	.295	.523	576	170	32	6	29	115	114	107	6
1939		8	.143	.143	28	4	0	0	0	2	1	5	0
17 yrs.		2164	.340	.632	8001	2721	535	162	493	1888	1990	1508	102
				3rd							7th	3rd	
WORLD SERIES													
1926	NY A	7	.348	.435	23	8	2	0	0	1	3	5	0
1927		4	.308	.769	13	4	2	2	0	2	5	3	0
1928		4	.545	1.727	11	6	1	0	4	5	9	6	0
1932		4	.529	1.118	17	9	1	0	3	9	8	2	0
1936		6	.292	.583	24	7	1	0	2	5	7	3	0
1937		5	.294	.647	17	5	1	1	1	4	3	5	0
1938		4	.286	.286	14	4	0	0	0	4	0	2	0
7 yrs.		34	.361	.731	119	43	8	3	10	30	35	26	0
			8th	3rd		9th	6th	4th	5th	4th	3rd	5th	

BABE RUTH

Yr.	Team	G	BA	SA	AB	H	2B	3B	HR	R	RBI	BB	SB
1914	Bos A	5	.200	.300	10	2	1	0	0	1	0	0	0
1915		42	.315	.576	92	29	10	1	4	16	21	9	0
1916		67	.272	.419	136	37	5	3	3	18	16	10	0
1917		52	.325	.472	123	40	6	3	2	14	12	12	0
1918		95	.300	.555	317	95	26	11	11	50	66	57	6
1919		130	.322	.657	432	139	34	12	29	103	114	101	7
1920	NY A	142	.376	.847	458	172	36	9	54	158	137	148	14
1921		152	.378	.846	540	204	44	16	59	177	171	144	17
1922		110	.315	.672	406	128	24	8	35	94	99	84	2
1923		152	.393	.764	522	205	45	13	41	151	131	170	17
1924		153	.378	.739	529	200	39	7	46	143	121	142	9
1925		98	.290	.543	359	104	12	2	25	61	66	59	2
1926		152	.372	.737	495	184	30	5	47	139	145	144	11
1927		151	.356	.772	540	192	29	8	60	158	164	138	7
1928		154	.323	.709	536	173	29	8	54	163	142	135	4
1929		135	.345	.697	499	172	26	6	46	121	154	72	5
1930		145	.359	.732	518	186	28	9	49	150	153	136	10
1931		145	.373	.700	534	199	31	3	46	149	163	128	5
1932		133	.341	.661	457	156	13	5	41	120	137	130	2
1933		137	.301	.582	459	138	21	3	34	97	103	114	4
1934		125	.288	.537	365	105	17	4	22	78	84	103	1
1935	BOS N	28	.181	.431	72	13	0	0	6	13	12	20	0
22 yrs.		2503	.342	.690	8399	2873	506	136	714	2174	2211	2056	123
				1st					2nd	2nd	2nd	1st	

BABE RUTH (CON'T)

Yr.	Team	G	BA	SA	AB	H	2B	3B	HR	R	RBI	BB	SB
WORLD SERIES													
1915	BOS A	1	.000	.000	1	0	0	0	0	0	0	0	0
1916		1	.000	.000	5	0	0	0	0	0	1	0	0
1918		3	.200	.600	5	1	0	1	0	0	2	0	0
1921	NY A	6	.313	.500	16	5	0	0	1	3	4	5	2
1922		5	.118	.176	17	2	1	0	0	1	1	2	0
1923		6	.368	1.000	19	7	1	1	3	8	3	8	0
1926		7	.300	.900	20	6	0	0	4	6	5	11	1
1927		4	.400	.800	15	6	0	0	2	4	7	2	1
1928		4	.625	1.375	16	10	3	0	3	9	4	1	0
1932		4	.333	.733	15	5	0	0	2	6	6	4	0
10 yrs.		41	.326	.744	129	42	5	2	15	37	33	33	4
		10th		2nd		10th			2nd	3rd	4th	2nd	

THE LEGENDARY 1927 TEAM WAS A HARD ACT TO FOLLOW. AP/WIDE WORLD

The

Thirties

IN A WAY, 1930 WAS A CHANGING
OF THE GUARD. NOT ONLY DID
1930 mark the end of the Roaring
Twenties, but it also marked the end
of big money in the stock market,
after the crash in 1929 that brought
on the Great Depression. And in baseball,
1929 marked the end of the Miller Huggins

era with his death on September 5.

Were the glory days of the 1920s over for the Yankees, too? At the beginning of the decade it seemed they had peaked and were now on the downside of the mountain. But by 1939 they had clinched their fifth World Series of the decade! There were bright moments throughout. For example, the great Lou Gehrig had his most productive game on June 3, 1932, when he hit 4 consecutive home runs against the Philadelphia Athletics. Then, in his fifth at-bat, in the ninth inning, he hit the longest shot of the day. But it wasn't a home run. He was gypped when Al Simmons caught it in deep center. Gehrig's timing for his greatest game was all wrong. John J. McGraw, the New York Giants manager for thirty-one years, retired on that day. All eyes in New York were focused on McGraw—not on the Iron Horse.

In 1932 the Yanks took the pennant and went on to trounce the Chicago Cubs in the World Series. This Series is memorable because of Ruth's famous "called shot" off Charlie Root in the fifth inning of Game 3— a homer after 2 strikes with the score tied, 4–4.

During the 1930s, things had fallen apart between Gehrig and Ruth, the two who had spent so many productive years together. The trouble went back to 1929, when they had got into an argument over salary. Ruth wanted Gehrig to join him in holding out for more money, but Gehrig, ever frugal, didn't want to risk losing what he had. And so a schism developed. Soon the two were barely talking.

Ruth was getting old and he knew it. His career as a player had wound down and he wanted to stay in baseball, be a manager, run a team. The Babe asked Ruppert to let him manage the Yankees, but Ruppert said no. Then Ruth was offered a player contract by the Boston Braves and left the Yankees in February 1935. But no one ever let him manage a team—and he retired from the game, a frustrated ex-ballplayer.

Gehrig in 1934 had a Triple Crown season and his stats continued high. He was part of the four World Series that the Yanks won in a row between 1936 and 1939, hitting a decent .294 in the 1937 Series. But in the 1938 World Series he hit only 4 singles in 14 at-bats—his worst performance ever.

On May 2, 1939, he asked to be taken out of the lineup and benched. In June at the Mayo Clinic he learned he had amyotropic lateral sclerosis—deterioration of the central nervous system—which took on the name Lou Gehrig's Disease.

July 4, 1939, was Lou Gehrig Appreciation Day at Yankee Stadium, where to more than 60,000 fans he delivered his emotional farewell "Luckiest Man on Earth" speech. The Babe was there and the two were warm to each other. The Iron Horse stayed as a non-player with the team for the rest of the season and lived until he was thirty-seven, dying on June 2, 1941.

Q. Jacob Ruppert had a favorite name for his favorite player, Babe Ruth. What did Ruppert call Ruth?

A. He called him "Root." Or at least it sounded like "root"—since Ruppert's slight German accent made the "th"s sound like "t"s.

• "Goodbye, Baseball" •

This is part of the farewell Lou Gehrig delivered to his devoted fans on July 4, 1939, on Lou Gehrig Appreciation Day: "For weeks I have been reading in the newspapers that I am a fellow who got a tough break. I don't believe it. I have been a lucky guy. For sixteen years into every ballpark in which I have ever walked, I received nothing but kindness and encouragement. Mine has been a full life. . . . I have a wonderful wife, I have a wonderful mother and father, and wonderful friends and teammates. I have been privileged to play many years with the famous Yankees, the greatest team of all times. . . . I may have been given a bad break, but I have an awful lot to live for. All in all, I can say on this day that I consider myself the luckiest man on the face of the earth."

With Ruth gone and Gehrig on his way out, a new star was needed. Joe DiMaggio fit the bill perfectly. Coming on board in 1936, DiMaggio was heralded the most all-around baseball player of all time. The Yankee Clipper was, according to his favorite manager, Joe McCarthy—for whom he played from 1936 through 1946—"the complete player" and "the best base runner I ever saw. He could have stolen fifty, sixty bases a year if I had let him."

But it was much more than base stealing that made DiMaggio the all-around player he was. He had great control as a batter; he could hit for average distances and could power the ball if need be. His instincts kicked in at center field; he knew the spot the ball would drop the moment it left the batter's bat. His superb throwing arm never missed its target, he never let the ball slip, or tossed it to the wrong base. He was a mar-

JOE DIMAGGIO. GLOBE PHOTOS, INC. **41**

velous base runner, daring and at the same time always alert. Aware every second of the other players in the field, he never missed a sign. From the beginning he was a natural team leader.

His career spanned thirteen years of playing ball with the Yanks from 1936 to 1942, with time out for military service (1943–1945), and then back again with the Yankees from 1946 to 1951. During his career he consistently broke records that had held up for years and established records that were hard for future players to break.

When DiMaggio was in the game, he always gave 100 percent—always. He was the Yankees team leader during years when they won 10 American League pennants and 9 World Championships.

He was 6′2″, and weighed about 193 pounds—a slim, tall, graceful man, whose every move was poetry in motion. To see him hit balls was something else. He had great talent, he played the game with honesty and integrity, and his genius glowed in his actions.

In spite of being a charismatic, stellar player on the field, he was a quiet and very shy man off the field. He deliberately avoided publicity and kept away from strangers. But his shyness did not bother his fans, who were legion—it added an almost magical quality to him.

Born in Martinez, California, he grew up playing on sandlots, then began playing professionally with the

San Francisco Seals of the Pacific Coast League. In 1933, when he was nineteen, he had a hitting streak of 61 games—the longest in professional ball history. In 1935 he was named Pacific Coast League MVP, batting .398 with 34 home runs and 154 RBIs.

Jacob Ruppert called in DiMaggio for an extensive interview and hired him at $25,000 a season. In 1936, in his first major league game with the Yankees, the Yankee Clipper had 3 hits—a triple and a pair of singles. In a game played June 24, 1936, he hit 2 homers in 1 inning. On August 27, 1938, he had 3 triples in one game. In a doubleheader on July 13, 1940, he batted in nine runners. On September 10, 1950, DiMaggio became the first man to hit 3 home runs in a game played at Washington's Griffith Stadium. In his lifetime stats, he hit 3 homers in a single game three times.

He had an incredible hitting streak in 1941, batting safely in 56 consecutive games—a stupendous record that still stands. His batting average for 1939 was .381, the second highest in Yankee history. At the end of his career he had almost as many home runs as he had strikeouts—361 to 369. On average, he struck out once every 18.18 at-bats, and homered once for every 18.84 at bats.

At decade's end Ruth was gone, Gehrig was gone. Jake Ruppert, who had seen the team surge and wane, died on January 13, 1939. Ed Barrow, a trustee of his estate, was elected club president. The old guard had departed, and there was a new guard standing in its place. The Yankees were on the verge of a long and successful World Series drive through the forties, fifties, and sixties before they tapered off into the 3–10 seventies, the miserable 1–10 eighties, and the 1–6 nineties.

• "DiMaggio's Two Loves" •

Joe DiMaggio loved baseball, he loved the Yankees and its personnel, and he loved the pinstripe uniform. But he was known for more than baseball when, after his retire-

ment in 1951, he married Marilyn Monroe.
They divorced soon after. Still, in 1993, when
making a trip to Italy with the Italian-
American Foundation to visit his parents'
hometown, the Yankee Clipper was mobbed at
the airport in Rome—not for having been a
Yankee but for having been the husband of
Marilyn Monroe.

DIMAGGIO WITH HIS Other LOVE, MARILYN MONROE. GLOBE PHOTOS, INC.

The
Forties

. . . .

THE NEW YORK YANKEES CONTIN-
UED THEIR DOMINATION OF THE
major leagues in baseball through the
1940s, even as the United States became involved in World War II on a
two-continent front. The Yanks won
the American pennant in 1941 and the World
Series as well; it lost the Series in 1942, but

took it again in 1943 and 1947. The unevenness of their victories and defeats had a great deal to do with the war effort and its effect on the team's personnel.

1941 was a memorable year for the Yanks—Joe DiMaggio, with 30 home runs, 125 RBIs, and a batting average of .357, hit safely in 56 consecutive games. Ironically, the streak began on the day the Yanks lost their eighth game out of ten. The *New York Journal-American* headline read: "YANK ATTACK WEAKEST IN YEARS." This year was also memorable for the addition of talented shortstop Phil Rizzuto.

The 1943 season stands out not for the players who played and won, but for the number of players who did *not* play, including Joe DiMaggio, Phil Rizzuto, Tommy Henrich, Buddy Hassett, and Red Ruffing, all of whom were regulars serving in the military. The stars were gone, but

PHIL RIZZUTO BROUGHT TALENT AND DETERMINATION TO THE YANKS. PHOTOFEST

Q. To date, who has had the longest tenure as manager of the Yankees?

A. Joe McCarthy (1931–1946).

the Yanks still kept winning— in fact, they won 23 games by the margin of 1 run, and lost 23 by the same margin.

So many players were out in 1944 that the Yankees dropped to third place. In 1945 they were in fifth place—the worst they'd scored since 1925.

After the Japanese attack on Pearl Harbor, President Franklin D. Roosevelt had stated: "I honestly feel it would be best for the country to keep baseball going. These players are a definite recreational asset to their fellow citizens—and that, in my judgment, is thoroughly worthwhile." The game went on.

Phil Rizzuto proved a well-needed standout during the last half of the forties. Born in Brooklyn, Phil Rizzuto graduated from Richmond Hill High School in 1936 and tried out for the Dodgers and the Giants. Both teams said that at 5′6″ and 150 pounds, he was too small to play baseball. Casey Stengel, then manager of the Dodgers, and often short on tact, was less than subtle in his opinion of Rizzuto's playing baseball, telling him to go get a shoe shine box. That was one of the reasons Stengel was never Rizzuto's favorite manager (Joe McCarthy was).

Other managers felt the same way Stengel did, however, and remained adamant about Rizzuto's shrimpish size. He was forced to work his way up through the minor leagues, starting with the Yankees in their farm system in the same year he graduated from high school. He was making about $75 a month then, playing in Bassett, Virginia, and then in Norfolk, and in Kansas City in 1939.

In Norfolk he had hit .336 in 1938, and in Kansas .316 in 1939, and .347 in 1940 against top-notch minor league pitching. In the minors he really sharpened his abilities at the double play. In Kansas City, he worked with Gerry Priddy in what was called probably the best double-play duo in minor league history.

In 1941 he and Priddy were invited to try out for the Yanks, and both made the club. By then, his talents honed by his years in the minors, Rizzuto was in almost peak form. He was then able to prove conclusively that his diminutive size had nothing to do with his talent and ability.

Rizzuto was a regular with the Yankees from 1941 through 1956, except for three years (1943–1945) spent in the U.S. Navy. His stats were always impressive. In 1950 he collected 200 hits during the season— still a club record for a shortstop. Ty Cobb once said that only two players, Phil Rizzuto and Stan Musial, would have been stars in Cobb's time. He included Rizzuto's exceptional ability to hit to any field, and to lay down a bunt where it was most effective, plus his all-round defensive genius. Rizzuto led the major league stats in sacrifice hits for four straight years from 1949 through 1952.

Joe McCarthy said of him, "For a little fellow to beat a big fellow he has to be terrific, he has to have everything, and Rizzuto's got it." McCarthy saw that Rizzuto brought that talent and determination to the Yanks. Tommy Henrich said, "We have nothing to worry about as long as Rizzuto remains healthy. He's the team's spark plug."

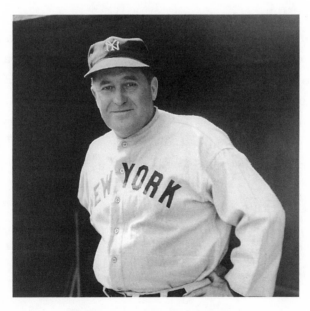

MANAGER JOE MCCARTHY. GLOBE PHOTOS, INC.

His competition had him well scouted. Boston's Ted Williams once pointed to Rizzuto in the field and told Tommy Henrich, "If we had that little squirt, we'd be out in front by ten games now."

The Scooter was a double-threat player—as great with defensive plays as with offensive plays. In 1951 in a game late in the season, Cleveland's Jim Hegan hit a fly between left field and the infield. Rizzuto ran out into shallow left and, with his back to the plate, grabbed the ball in the air with his bare hand. He stumbled badly, went down, and rolled into foul territory—still gripping the ball.

He was formidable, too, at the double play. He worked it with five different Yankee second basemen: Joe "Flash" Gordon, Snuffy Stirnweiss, Jerry Coleman, Billy Martin, and Gil McDougald. His athletic ability, his grace, his astute knowledge of the dynamics of the game, all made him a super player by any consideration.

In spite of his earlier pronouncement, Casey Stengel later said: "He is the greatest shortstop I have ever seen in my entire baseball career, and I have watched some beauties. Honus Wagner was a better hitter, sure, but I've seen this kid make plays Wagner never did. If I were a retired gentleman, I would follow the Yankees around just to see Rizzuto work those miracles every day."

In 1946 another player who became a star—and a most colorful superstar at that—joined the Yankees. His name was Lawrence Peter Berra.

He grew up on the Hill, a poor Italian section in St. Louis, Missouri, playing sandlot ball with his buddies. When they were kids, one of them, Bobby Hofman (who also made it to the majors), gave Berra his nickname "Yogi" from an Indian yogi they saw in a movie who Hofman thought looked and walked like Berra. And the name stuck for life.

When he tried out for them, both the St. Louis Browns and the St. Louis Cardinals gave Berra the cold shoulder. Browns: not up to snuff. Cardinals: too awkward and slow to play. Branch Rickey, the Cardinals skipper, said, "You'll never be a ballplayer. Take my advice, son, and forget about baseball. Get into some other line of business."

The Yankees had no such reservations about him. In 1943 they signed him to a $90-a-month contract to

PHIL RIZZUTO ON YOGI BERRA'S ABILITIES AS A CATCHER: "IN RECENT YEARS THERE HAS BEEN A TENDENCY TO RATE BERRA AS THE SECOND-BEST HITTING CATCHER OF THE MODERN ERA—BEHIND JOHNNY BENCH. I HAVE ALWAYS FOUND THIS COMPARISON PUZZLING. BERRA LEADS BENCH IN BATTING AVERAGE BY NEARLY 20 POINTS AS WELL AS IN RBIS AND TOTAL RUNS SCORED, DESPITE THE FACT THAT YOGI HAD FEWER AT-BATS. BENCH LEADS ONLY IN TOTAL HOME RUNS AND TIES BERRA FOR TOTAL AVERAGE. AS FOR YOGI'S OVERALL CONTRIBUTION TO HIS TEAM, YOGI'S TEAMS OUTPERFORMED BENCH'S."

play for the Norfolk farm club of the Piedmont League, where Berra hit 7 homers, 56 RBIs, and batted .253 in 111 games. Yogi Berra signed on with the U.S. Navy in 1944, and in 1946 was playing for the Yankees Newark Club where he batted .314, hit 15 homers, 59 RBIs, in 277 at-bats.

Late in the 1946 season he joined the Yankees; playing in only 7 games, he hit .364. In his very first major league at-bat, he hit a home run at Yankee Stadium off Jesse Flores of the Athletics. The following year he caught 51 games and played 24 games in the outfield. In 1948 he caught 71 games

YOGI BERRA STOOD OUT ON THE YANKEES AS
A PLAYER, THEN A COACH AND MANAGER.
GLOBE PHOTOS, INC./BOB PRESTON

and played 50 games as an outfielder. From 1949 to 1959 he was a regular Yankee catcher. From 1960 to 1962, he played catcher and left field. In 1963 he was a catcher and pinch hitter. Except for 4 games with the Mets in 1965, he played his entire career with the Yankees.

Yogi Berra was an indefatigable player. His stats showed a total of 8,711 putouts and 9,619 chances behind the plate, ranking him fifth of all catchers in baseball history. He caught 1,696 games, ranking him seventh in baseball history. He was one of only four catchers to field 1.000 for a season (1958). He made two unassisted double plays as a catcher—another American League record—June 15, 1947, against the Browns, and August 17, 1962, against the Athletics. He batted in 30 homers in 1952 and 1956, the most ever hit by a catcher in the American League. His 313 homers hit as a catcher is the American League record for catchers. He played on 10 World Championship teams—another record no one else in baseball history has beaten. Every season between 1948 and 1962 he was selected for the American League team for the All-Star Game, hitting a homer in the 1959 game. Berra has played in more World Series—14—than anyone else. He played 75 World Series games and had 259 at-bats, and 10 doubles. He hit at least 1 home run in 9 World Series, a record he held with Mickey Mantle. He knocked in at least 1 run in 11 Series, a Series record. He scored a run in 12 Series, another record. He walked at least once in 13 Series. He also threw out 36 attempted base stealers in Series play—yet another Series record.

Berra studied hard to become a great catcher. At first Casey Stengel, the Yankee manager, called the pitches for him. But by 1952, he was doing it all himself. And he was proving to be a very hard man to shave. Most ballplayers will admit that no one could touch Yogi Berra as a signal caller. His main claims to fame were the three no-hitters he called—two of them by Allie Reynolds in 1951, and the other the perfect game tossed by Don Larsen in the 1956 World Series. To Reynolds and Larsen, no other catcher ever called a better game than Berra.

Berra, one of the best-seasoned catchers in the business, became more than a baseball player after he was in the public eye as a man whose "sayings" were funny, irrepressible, and at the same time, uncannily incisive. Probably his most famous line was "It ain't over till it's over."

In 1945, while the war was still on, a group of three men—Larry MacPhail, Dan Topping, and Del Webb—purchased the Yankees from the heirs of Jacob

Ruppert. Their next important move was to hire an aging reprobate named Casey Stengel in 1948 as their manager. It was Stengel who brought on the postwar boom in Yankee fortunes.

• "It Ain't Over Till It's Over" •

The press loved to quote Yogi Berra. He was credited with saying, "You can see a lot just by observing," "If you come to a fork in the road, take it," and "Why buy good luggage? You only use it when you travel." Berra's comments became so legendary that he was given credit for things he never said—like, "It's déjà vu all over again." He also did *not* telegraph Johnny Bench when Bench broke one of Berra's records: "Congratulations. I knew the record would stand until it was broken." Still, what he did say made him an icon.

PHIL RIZZUTO

Yr.	Team	G	BA	SA	AB	H	2B	3B	HR	R	RBI	BB	SB
1941	NY A	133	.307	.398	515	158	20	9	3	65	46	27	14
1942		144	.284	.374	553	157	24	7	4	79	68	44	22
1946		126	.257	.310	471	121	17	1	2	53	38	34	14
1947		153	.273	.364	549	150	26	9	2	78	60	57	11
1948		128	.252	.328	464	117	13	2	6	65	50	60	6
1949		153	.275	.358	614	169	22	7	5	110	64	72	18
1950		155	.324	.439	617	200	36	7	7	125	66	92	12
1951		144	.274	.346	540	148	21	6	2	87	43	58	18
1952		152	.254	.341	578	147	24	10	2	89	43	67	17
1953		134	.271	.351	413	112	21	3	2	54	54	71	4
1954		127	.195	.251	307	60	11	0	2	47	15	41	3
1955		81	.259	.322	143	37	4	1	1	19	9	22	7
1956		31	.231	.231	52	12	0	0	0	6	6	6	3
13 yrs.		1661	.273	.355	5816	1588	239	62	38	877	562	651	149
WORLD SERIES													
1941	NY A	5	.111	.111	18	2	0	0	0	0	0	3	1
1942		5	.381	.524	21	8	0	0	1	2	1	2	2
1947		7	.308	.346	26	8	1	0	0	3	2	4	2
1949		5	.167	.167	18	3	0	0	0	2	1	3	1
1950		4	.143	.143	14	2	0	0	0	1	0	3	1
1951		6	.320	.440	25	8	0	0	1	5	3	2	0
1952		7	.148	.185	27	4	1	0	0	2	0	5	0
1953		6	.316	.368	19	6	1	0	0	4	0	3	1
1955		7	.267	.267	15	4	0	0	0	2	1	5	2
9 yrs.		52	.246	.295	183	45	3	0	2	21	8	30	10
		6th			7th	7th					10th		4th	3rd

JOE DIMAGGIO

Yr.	Team	G	BA	SA	AB	H	2B	3B	HR	R	RBI	BB	SB
1936	NY A	138	.323	.576	637	206	44	15	29	132	125	24	4
1937		151	.346	.673	621	215	35	15	46	151	167	64	3
1938		145	.324	.581	599	194	32	13	32	129	140	59	6
1939		120	.381	.671	462	176	32	6	30	108	126	52	3
1940		132	.352	.626	508	179	28	9	31	93	133	61	1
1941		139	.357	.643	541	193	43	11	30	122	125	76	4
1942		154	.305	.498	610	186	29	13	21	123	114	68	4
1946		132	.290	.511	503	146	20	8	25	81	95	59	1
1947		141	.315	.522	534	168	31	10	20	97	97	64	3
1948		153	.320	.598	594	190	26	11	39	110	155	67	1
1949		76	.346	.596	272	94	14	6	14	58	67	55	0
1950		139	.301	.585	525	158	33	10	32	114	122	80	0
1951		116	.263	.422	415	109	22	4	12	72	71	61	0
13 yrs.		1736	.325	.579	6821	2214	389	131	361	1390	1537	790	30
				6th									
WORLD SERIES													
1936	NY A	6	.346	.462	26	9	3	0	0	3	3	1	0
1937		5	.273	.409	22	6	0	0	1	2	4	0	0
1938		4	.267	.467	15	4	0	0	1	4	2	1	0
1939		4	.313	.500	16	5	0	0	1	3	3	1	0
1941		5	.263	.263	19	5	0	0	0	1	1	2	0
1942		5	.333	.333	21	7	0	0	0	3	3	0	0
1947		7	.231	.462	26	6	0	0	2	4	5	6	0
1949		5	.111	.278	18	2	0	0	1	2	2	3	0
1950		4	.308	.615	13	4	1	0	1	2	2	3	0
1951		6	.261	.478	23	6	2	0	1	3	5	2	0
10 yrs.		51	.271	.422	199	54	6	0	8	27	30	19	0
		7th			3rd	4th			7th	5th	5th	10th	

YOGI BERRA

Yr.	Team	G	BA	SA	AB	H	2B	3B	HR	R	RBI	BB	SB
1946	NY A	7	.364	.682	22	8	1	0	2	3	4	1	0
1947		83	.280	.464	293	82	15	3	11	41	54	13	0
1948		125	.305	.488	469	143	24	10	14	70	98	25	3
1949		116	.277	.480	415	115	20	2	20	59	91	22	2
1950		151	.322	.533	597	192	30	6	28	116	124	55	4
1951		141	.294	.492	547	161	19	4	27	92	88	44	5
1952		142	.273	.478	534	146	17	1	30	97	98	66	2
1953		137	.296	.523	503	149	23	5	27	80	108	50	0
1954		151	.307	.488	584	179	28	6	22	88	125	56	0
1955		147	.272	.470	541	147	20	3	27	84	108	60	1
1956		140	.298	.534	521	155	29	2	30	93	105	65	3
1957		134	.251	.438	482	121	14	2	24	74	82	57	1
1958		122	.266	.471	433	115	17	3	22	60	90	35	3
1959		131	.284	.462	472	134	25	1	19	64	69	43	1
1960		120	.276	.446	359	99	14	1	15	46	62	38	2
1961		119	.271	.466	395	107	11	0	22	62	61	35	2
1962		86	.224	.388	232	52	8	0	10	25	35	24	0
1963		64	.293	.497	147	43	6	0	8	20	28	15	1
1965	NY N	4	.222	.222	9	2	0	0	0	1	0	0	0
19 yrs.		2120	.285	.482	7555	2150	321	49	358	1175	1430	704	30

YOGI BERRA (CON'T)

Yr.	Team	G	BA	SA	AB	H	2B	3B	HR	R	RBI	BB	SB
WORLD SERIES													
1947	NY A	6	.158	.316	19	3	0	0	1	2	2	1	0
1949		4	.063	.063	16	1	0	0	0	2	1	1	0
1950		4	.200	.400	15	3	0	0	1	2	2	2	0
1951		6	.261	.304	23	6	1	0	0	4	0	2	0
1952		7	.214	.464	28	6	1	0	2	2	3	2	0
1953		6	.429	.619	21	9	1	0	1	3	4	3	0
1955		7	.417	.583	24	10	1	0	1	5	2	3	0
1956		7	.360	.800	25	9	2	0	3	5	10	4	0
1957		7	.320	.480	25	8	1	0	1	5	2	4	0
1958		7	.222	.333	27	6	3	0	0	3	2	1	0
1960		7	.318	.455	22	7	0	0	1	6	8	2	0
1961		4	.273	.545	11	3	0	0	1	2	3	5	0
1962		2	.000	.000	2	0	0	0	0	0	0	2	0
1963		1	.000	.000	1	0	0	0	0	0	0	0	0
14 yrs.		75	.274	.452	259	71	10	0	12	41	39	32	0
		1st			1st	1st	1st		3rd	2nd	2nd	3rd	

MANAGER CASEY STENGEL. GLOBE PHOTOS, INC.

The Fabulous
Fifties

· · · · · · · ·  · · · · · · · ·

HE WAS PACKAGED ALL WRONG. CASEY STENGEL, THE MAN WHO would be the prime mover of the 1950s Yankees team, looked like a stand-up comedian ready to do undignified pratfalls in a vaudeville routine.

Stengel was a raunchy, die-hard fifty-nine-year-old when he became manager in 1948.

STENGEL ATTENDED DENTAL SCHOOL IN HIS HOME TOWN OF KANSAS CITY. BUT HE NEVER PULLED A TOOTH!

Under his twelve-year management, the Yankees won 10 American League pennants, and 5 consecutive World Series (1949–1953). The Yankees also acquired a number of blockbuster baseball stars under him—names etched forever in the Yankee pantheon of players: Allie Reynolds, Eddie Lopat, Vic Raschi, Whitey Ford, Mickey Mantle, Billy Martin, Elston Howard.

And in 1956, in the middle of the Decade of Stengel, Don Larsen pitched a no-hitter in a World Series game that will be remembered by all baseball fans for eternity.

Casey Stengel loved baseball. He started as an outfielder in the minor leagues—Kankakee, Maysville, Aurora, Montgomery—before joining the Brooklyn Dodgers in 1912. The next fourteen seasons found Stengel with the Dodgers, the Pirates, the Phillies, the Giants, and finally, the Braves.

He batted .284 lifetime and .393 for 3 World Series. In the 1923 World Series, he hit 2 game-winning home runs for the Giants against their rivals the Yankees. They were the first 2 homers hit in the new Yankee Stadium—an ironic and prophetic note for later Yankee fans who came to revere Casey.

In 1925 he moved out of playing and into managing, buying a piece of the Worcester, Massachusetts, Eastern League club and becoming president, general manager, and player-manager. In 1926, he left to manage Toledo, winning the American Association pennant in 1927. He returned to Brooklyn to coach in 1932 and in 1934 was named the Dodgers manager.

Then came Boston; he managed the Braves from 1938 to 1943, when he moved again, this time to Milwaukee. Stengel's first taste of the Yankees came when George Weiss, the general manager of the club, hired him to manage the Yankee Kansas City farm team. His next stint managing three seasons on the Oakland Oaks of the Pacific Coast League was so successful that he was named Minor League Manager of the Year in 1948 by *The Sporting News*.

Stengel managed the Yanks like Captain Queeg on the bridge of the minesweeper *Caine*, manipulating his players like chessmen on a board. His platoon system sometimes worked seven first basemen, one after the other, in various combinations. Only Stengel could unravel it. He was rough on the guys who goofed up, and he loved the guys who finished first.

One of the first great players to appear on Stengel's Yankee roster was Whitey Ford. Edward Charles Ford was a New York product, growing up in the Astoria section of Queens. As early as 1946—Ford was only a teenager—he was paid $7,000 to play in the minor leagues for the Yanks, and just four years later he was called up to the show.

And what a job he did in 1950. He won 9 out of 10

WHITEY FORD WAS KNOWN FOR THROWING A GREAT VARIETY OF PITCHES.
BOB MORELAND/GLOBE PHOTOS, INC.

games, saving the pennant for the Yanks that year. After that winning season, he joined the military and missed the years 1951–1953.

Returning in 1953, Whitey, also nicknamed "Chairman of the Board," settled down to become one of the star pitchers of the whole Yankee organization. His pitches were a rare and exotic assortment of throws

THE PRESS IDOLIZED STENGEL. LATER ON IN HIS LIFE, WHEN HE WAS HIRED TO MANAGE THE LOSING-WAYS NEW YORK METS, HE MADE ONE OF HIS MOST QUOTABLE QUOTES WHEN HE ASKED THE TEAM: "CAN'T ANYBODY HERE PLAY THIS GAME?"

of all kinds. Up and down. In and out. Changed speeds. He had a fastball whenever he needed it. He had a curveball as baffling as any good pitcher's. He had other trick pitches and was said occasionally to throw the illegal spitball and a "mudball"—a ball doctored by having mud rubbed into its seams. Later he picked up on the slider, a pitch he didn't throw regularly until after 1961.

Although some people underrated Whitey as a fielding pitcher, he had maybe the finest pickoff move to first base in the history of the game—a screen of camouflage moves hiding his real feints that fooled many a man trying to get the jump on him to second base.

Whitey Ford was inducted into the Hall of Fame in 1974—with his famed 1950s teammate Mickey Mantle. Mantle represented the prototypical American suc-

ON OCTOBER 6, 1965,
WHITEY BEAT THE RED SOX,
9–7, FOR HIS 232ND VIC-
TORY AS A YANKEE
PITCHER—MAKING HIM
THE MOST WINNING
YANKEE PITCHER IN HIS-
TORY.

cess story. A man who came from nowhere, he achieved great fame in baseball history, then from there went on to become a national legend. He *looked* the part, that go-to-hell grin on his face, that graceful walk of his, that devilish twinkle in his eye as he played dumb tricks on his teammates.

The man who made Mantle into the player he would become was his father, Mutt Mantle, a zinc miner in Oklahoma. A baseball nut, who decided that his son would be a major league ballplayer, Mantle named Mickey after his favorite player in 1931—Mickey Cochrane.

Mutt Mantle knew the value of a left-handed hitter, and he deliberately developed his son into a switch-hitter who could bat from both sides of the plate. By the time young Mantle began playing ball, he was adept at both left and right hitting. Mickey's job as a teenager, mining zinc with his father four hundred feet underground, helped him develop tremendous muscles in his arms—which came in handy later on for slamming the ball out of the field when a solid pitch crossed the plate.

The Yankee scouts saw him playing semiprofessional ball in Commerce, Oklahoma, liked what they saw, and signed him in 1949 for a $1,100 bonus and

$400 for playing the rest of the season. He had a good season at shortstop in the minors, and by the end of 1950 he was traveling with the Yanks, but he was not on the roster.

Stengel moved him to the outfield, which was quite a switch from shortstop, and with the help of Stengel, Joe DiMaggio, and Tommy Henrich, Mantle learned to play the position. After starting the 1951 season in the majors, Mantle revitalized his hitting stats back on the farm team, returning to finish the season. He played 96 games with a batting average of .267, and came through with 13 homers and 65 RBIs. During 1951, he played right field next to Joe DiMaggio, who was in his last

MICKEY MANTLE—THE YANKEE SCOUTS LIKED WHAT THEY SAW. JOE TRAVER/GAMMA LIAISON

season as center field for the Yanks. When DiMaggio retired, Stengel moved Mantle into center field, where he played from 1952 to 1966.

Switch-hitting was Mantle's forte. "Ted Williams was a real hitter," he once said. "Me, I just got up there and swung for the roof ever' time and waited to see what would happen."

His home runs were spectacular drives. The Yankees began measuring them with a tape measure and publicizing his longest ones. On June 21, 1955, he hit the first home run in Yankee Stadium to go over the black screen. Hit to the right of the 461-foot sign, the ball landed in the bleachers, 486 feet from home plate. Nearly ten years later, on August 12, 1964, he hit the longest homer ever measured inside Yankee Stadium. Batting left-handed against Chicago's Ray Herbert, he got a 502-foot hit—he drove the ball over the 461-foot sign in center field. And he could hit them on away games too: At Griffith Stadium, Washington, batting right-handed, in 1953, he hit a 565-foot homer over the left field wall.

Mantle had huge seasons with the Yankees—.353, 52 homers, 130 RBIs, to win the Triple Crown in 1956. He worked 12 World Series in his first fourteen seasons.

Q. Who among the Yankees played in the most official ball games?

A. Mickey Mantle, with 2,401 games plus 65 World Series games—a total of 2,466.

He was a smart player. More than once he scored from second base on a wild pitch, and eight times he led the Yankees in stolen bases. His 5 inside-the-park homers stand as a tribute to his speed around the diamond and mark another club record. He also stole a remarkable 133 bases in 163 attempts during his first twelve seasons, an 8.16 percentage.

Mickey Mantle retired in 1969, returning annually on Old Timers' Day. The change from the zinc mine four hundred feet underground in Oklahoma to the dizzying heights of the Copacabana spilling drinks with Whitey Ford and Billy Martin had had its effect, however. He sunk into alcoholism. And he admitted after he retired: "Casey said, 'This guy's going to be better than DiMaggio.' It didn't happen. God gave me a great body, and I didn't take care of it." In 1995 he had a liver transplant; two months later he died from lung cancer.

Mantle first met pal Billy Martin when Martin joined the Yankees in 1950. From the minute he came on board, he looked like a natural to become one of the leaders of the team. When Joe DiMaggio—whom

Martin had become close to—left in 1951, Martin filled his place as a team leader. A Californian, he was an aggressive, cocky kid, always ready to fight at the drop of the hat, and oftentimes cooking up some scheme to get the team riled up.

Casey Stengel loved him—and used him as a kind of catalyst who could get things moving when the team seemed to slow down. He had scrapes with his fellow players, as well as with players on opposing teams, but it never seemed to hurt his popularity. In addition to friendships with DiMaggio and Mantle, Martin could add Whitey Ford, Yogi Berra, and Phil Rizzuto—the real guts of the club—to his list of fans.

Martin bounced back to the minors during his rookie season, but was a regular second baseman in 1952, 1953, and 1956. He served in the military from 1954 through most of 1955. He was a good second baseman and a wizard at turning double plays. His prowess during World Series games really made Martin notable: He was tied for fourth on the all-time Series list for triples (3). He had a lifetime World Series batting average of .333, making him fourth on the all-time list.

In the 1952 and 1953 World Series he made some excellent plays. In Game 2 of the 1952 World Series, he hit a 3-run homer and led the Yankees to a 7–1 win over Brooklyn. Then in Game 7, with 2 outs and the bases loaded, he nailed a wind-borne pop-up to save the entire Series for the Yankees. In the next year's Series, he was the hitting star (.500, 23 total bases—third most in Series history). And in the bottom of the ninth of Game 6, a single he hit decided the game, which gave the Yanks a fifth straight Series win.

His career as Yankee player was short-lived. George Weiss blamed Billy for a fight that broke out at the Copacabana Club in New York City in May 1957 between six Yankee players and a group of drunken bowlers, and used it as a reason to fire him.

The team was gearing up for a good run at the decade of the 1960s, having won 7 pennants in the 1950s, and 5 World Championships.

· "The Perfect Game" ·

Don Larsen was known around the Yankees as "Night Rider" because of his wide-ranging interest in bright lights and the after-dark life. After a four A.M. automobile accident he had, general manager George Weiss wanted to trade him off. Casey Stengel nixed the

DON LARSEN, FAMED FOR HIS 1956 WORLD SERIES NO-HITTER. CRANSTON & ELKINS/PHOTOFEST, 3/4/58

idea, responding to Weiss's question, "Why was Don out at four in the morning?" with "He was mailing a letter."

Larsen's no-hitter World Series game redeemed him—a bit. *The New York Times* headlined the feat: "The Imperfect Man Pitches the Perfect Game." Larsen put it another way. "Everybody's entitled to a good day."

In 1955 the Yankee color line was broken by the arrival of Elston Howard, a catcher, outfielder, and first baseman from St. Louis, Missouri. From the first, he hit it off with the mainstays of the Yankees—Mickey Mantle, Whitey Ford, Yogi Berra, and Phil Rizzuto—and had little trouble acclimating himself to the team. The top management was certainly prejudiced, however, particularly George Weiss. Even Casey Stengel made an occasional remark that smacked of racism.

Howard had to live with a black family in

the segregated part of town during his first spring training in St. Petersburg, Florida. He was the only player not allowed to stay at the hotel with the rest of the Yankees. Still, after making the Yanks roster in 1955, he was selected to play for the American League All-Star team for nine consecutive seasons (1957–1965). He was also the first black player to win the MVP Award in the American League, and the American League's first black coach—back at the Yankees in 1969.

MICKEY MANTLE

Yr.	Team	G	BA	SA	AB	H	2B	3B	HR	R	RBI	BB	SB
1951	NY A	96	.267	.443	341	91	11	5	13	61	65	43	8
1952		142	.311	.530	549	171	37	7	23	94	87	75	4
1953		127	.295	.497	461	136	24	3	21	105	92	79	8
1954		146	.300	.525	543	163	17	12	27	129	102	102	5
1955		147	.306	.611	517	158	25	11	37	121	99	113	8
1956		150	.353	.705	533	188	22	5	52	132	130	112	10
1957		144	.365	.665	474	173	28	6	34	121	94	146	16
1958		150	.304	.592	519	158	21	1	42	127	97	129	18
1959		144	.285	.514	541	154	23	4	31	104	75	94	21
1960		153	.275	.558	527	145	17	6	40	119	94	111	14
1961		153	.317	.687	514	163	16	6	54	132	128	126	12
1962		123	.321	.605	377	121	15	1	30	96	89	122	9
1963		65	.314	.622	172	54	8	0	15	40	35	40	2
1964		143	.303	.591	465	141	25	2	35	92	111	99	6
1965		122	.255	.452	361	92	12	1	19	44	46	73	4
1966		108	.288	.538	333	96	12	1	23	40	56	57	1
1967		144	.245	.434	440	108	17	0	22	63	55	107	1
1968		144	.237	.398	435	103	14	1	18	57	54	106	6
18 yrs.		2401	.298	.557	8102	2415	344	72	536	1677	1509	1734	153
									8th			5th	

MICKEY MANTLE (CON'T)

Yr.	Team	G	BA	SA	AB	H	2B	3B	HR	R	RBI	BB	SB
WORLD SERIES													
1951	NY A	2	.200	.200	5	1	0	0	0	1	0	2	0
1952		7	.345	.655	29	10	1	1	2	5	3	3	0
1953		6	.208	.458	24	5	0	0	2	3	7	3	0
1955		3	.200	.500	10	2	0	0	1	1	1	0	0
1956		7	.250	.667	24	6	1	0	3	6	4	6	1
1957		6	.263	.421	19	5	0	0	1	3	2	3	0
1958		7	.250	.583	24	6	0	1	2	4	3	7	0
1960		7	.400	.800	25	10	1	0	3	8	11	8	0
1961		2	.167	.167	6	1	0	0	0	0	0	0	0
1962		7	.120	.160	25	3	1	0	0	2	0	4	2
1963		4	.133	.333	15	2	0	0	1	1	1	1	0
1964		7	.333	.792	24	8	2	0	3	8	8	6	0
12 yrs.		65	.257	.535	230	59	6	2	18	42	40	43	3
		2nd			2nd	2nd				1st	1st	1st	1st

WHITEY FORD

Yr.	Team	W	L	PCT	ERA	G	GS	CG	IP	H	BB	SO
1950	NY A	9	1	.900	2.81	20	12	7	112	87	52	59
1953		18	6	.750	3.00	32	30	11	207	187	110	110
1954		16	8	.667	2.82	34	28	11	210.2	170	101	125
1955		18	7	.720	2.63	39	33	18	253.2	188	113	137
1956		19	6	.760	2.47	31	30	18	225.2	187	84	141
1957		11	5	.688	2.57	24	17	5	129.1	114	53	84
1958		14	7	.667	2.01	30	29	15	219.1	174	62	145
1959		16	10	.615	3.04	35	29	9	204	194	89	114
1960		12	9	.571	3.08	33	29	8	192.2	168	65	85
1961		25	4	.862	3.21	39	39	11	283	242	92	209
1962		17	8	.680	2.90	38	37	7	257.2	243	69	160
1963		24	7	.774	2.74	38	37	13	269.1	240	56	189
1964		17	6	.739	2.13	39	36	12	244.2	212	57	172
1965		16	13	.552	3.24	37	36	9	244.1	241	50	162
1966		2	5	.286	2.47	22	9	0	73	79	24	43
1967		2	4	.333	1.64	7	7	2	44	40	9	21
16 yrs.		236	106	.690 3rd	2.75	498	438	156	3170.1	2766	1086	1956

WORLD SERIES												
1950	NY A	1	0	1.000	0.00	1	1	0	8.2	7	1	7
1953		0	1	.000	4.50	2	2	0	8	9	2	7
1955		2	0	1.000	2.12	2	2	1	17	13	8	10
1956		1	1	.500	5.25	2	2	1	12	14	2	8
1957		1	1	.500	1.13	2	2	1	16	11	5	7
1958		0	1	.000	4.11	3	3	0	15.1	19	5	16
1960		2	0	1.000	0.00	2	2	2	18	11	2	8
1961		2	0	1.000	0.00	2	2	1	14	6	1	7
1962		1	1	.500	4.12	3	3	1	19.2	24	4	12
1963		0	2	.000	4.50	2	2	0	12	10	3	8
1964		0	1	.000	8.44	1	1	0	5.1	8	1	4
11 yrs.		10	8	.556	2.71	22	22	7	146	132	34	94
		1st	1st			1st	1st	4th	1st	1st	1st	1st

The Soporific
Sixties

THE 1960S WARMED FOR A BIG BANG EARLY ON—1961 WAS A STANDOUT year—but it was downhill from there. The 1960 season saw some good and some bad. Thanks to a rocking bullpen (and the surprising and aggressive changes implemented by Casey Stengel), the team made it to the Series. A devastating ninth-inning

Pirate home run, however, gave the final victory to Pittsburg in Game 7.

By the end of the year, management was in a tizzy, as the longtime rumor that 1960 would be Stengel's last season with the Yanks came true. He was "retired" on October 15. George Weiss followed on November 2.

CASEY STENGEL LEFT THE YANKS IN 1960, BUT HIS GREAT COACHING LIVED ON IN MICKEY MANTLE. GLOBE PHOTOS, INC.

Ralph Houk, also known as the "Major"—he had been a major in the Marines in World War II—took over for the departed Stengel. The team was together already. Houk simply led them, setting a regular rotation that worked. The Yanks won the Series in 1961 and 1962 under Houk.

There was no question about it: The Stengel era was over. Still, Stengel's work lingered on. He had signed on Roger Maris, a new slugger, at the beginning of the season. Maris, a left-handed power hitter who played a reasonable right field, earned impressive stats his first year (39 HRs, .283). In 1961, Maris was put to the test, as it were. Both he and Mickey Mantle had stunning hitting records—numbers that threatened Babe Ruth's home run record. The media presented it as a contest between Maris and Mantle—and Babe Ruth. Maris pulled ahead, but no one knew for sure whether the players had really set up a contest or if it was something dreamed up by the press corps.

The 1961 season was big-time homers for Maris. On August 22 he became the first player ever to hit 50 in August. In game 154 of the season, at Baltimore on September 20, he hit homer 59. Number 60 was off Oriole Jack Fisher on September 26 at Yankee Stadium. Then in the season's final game on October 1, again at Yankee Stadium, he hit number 61 off Red Sox pitcher Tracy Stallard. Irony would have it that Maris actually hit 62 homers during the year, but lost one to a game that was rained out officially.

Although Mantle had slowed down at 54 and had more or less given up the race, for all his stress and strain Roger Maris was not credited with breaking the Sultan of Swat's record. The commissioner of baseball, Ford Frick, decided that Babe Ruth's record had *not* been bested because the Babe had played a season of only 154 games while Maris had played a season of 161. Fans divided into two camps again, the camp supporting Maris's victory arguing that Frick was just favoring Ruth.

1961 was Roger Maris's year to win almost every

ROGER MARIS. GLOBE PHOTOS, INC.

sports award out there. Here are just four: *Sports Illustrated's* "Sportsman of the Year," "Male Athlete of the Year" by the Associated Press, MVP of the American League, "Man of the Year" by *Sport.*

Maris fractured his hand in May 1965, but he did not realize it until September. The fans were getting on him for his performance, which had gone downhill. In 1966 he told Manager Ralph Houk that he wanted to retire at the end of the season. Then, in December 1966, the Yankees traded him to the Cardi-

JOE PEPITONE. JACK STAGER/GLOBE PHOTOS, INC.

nals for Charley Smith. Maris played for the Cards until 1968, when he retired. On December 14, 1985, he died after a long fight with cancer.

The 1961 Yankees boasted an awesome team and a major injection of excitement with the Maris/Mantle home run rivalry. They won the American League pennant and easily beat the Cincinnati Reds in the World Series, 4–1. More pennant wins came in 1962, 1963, and 1964, with a World Series win in 1962.

• "Where's the Fire, Pepi?" •

A bright spot in the mid-1960s came with the fun and colorful first baseman Joe Pepitone. Joe loved to rile up the team. During the 1963 championship American League game, Joe began a brawl—it livened up the game considerably. He was also known for his water balloon fighting skills, trying to sneak out at night, and the infamous time he sprayed manager Tommy Gott with a fire extinguisher.

With disappointing losses in 1963 and 1964, something seemed to be happening to the Yankees. The team suddenly lost its luster. In 1964 Ralph Houk was kicked upstairs after the Dodgers won the 1963 World Series in a 4-game sweep. Then, to the surprise of almost everyone—in baseball as well as out of it—Yogi Berra was transformed from a player to a manager in place of Houk. Berra did the best he could, helping the team to the World Series in 1964. Their loss to the St. Louis Cardinals did nothing to revitalize the fans, or the players.

In a fast move that many questioned, Berra was thrown out and a guy named Johnny Keane, who had managed the St. Louis Cardinals in 1964, was in. Keane came in ready to go, but the timing was all wrong. He treated the players badly, alienating both the team and the fans. Both had loved Berra for the baseball player he was, and even if he didn't do the managing all that well, he was a familiar figure. Keane would never measure up—he wasn't even a New Yorker. The team no longer played as a unit.

The Yanks hit the skids and came in sixth in 1965, the lowest they had been since 1925. But worse was to come. In 1966 they came in dead last in the American League. Not only that, attendance was plummeting at an unprecedented rate. At one game they played against the White Sox, there were only 413 spectators visible at Yankee Stadium.

Then, in a complicated financial deal, Yankees president Dan Topping gave up his stock, leaving the club entirely to the Columbia Broadcasting System. Mike Burke, a fifty-year-old network exec, became Yankee president in September 1966, at the close of the Yankees most miserable season. It was like déjà vu all over again, as Yogi Berra had not said; Burke rehired Ralph Houk as manager, and Houk returned to the dugout. Lee MacPhail took over as GM. MacPhail had worked in the Yank's front office in the 1950s and was shocked to find the team's farm system in disarray. He and Houk set out to rebuild the Yankees.

MANTLE CONTINUED TO EARN THE GREATEST STATS OF THE DECADE, SURROUNDED BY PLAYERS WHO WERE TOPS IN THE FIELD. STILL THE YANKEES COULDN'T GET ANYTHING GOING. MANTLE HIT HIS 500TH CAREER HOME RUN IN A GAME AGAINST BALTIMORE AT THE STADIUM—AND THE YANKS BEAT BALTIMORE TO BOOT. BUT THE TEAM STILL FINISHED NINTH IN 1967, FIFTH IN 1968, AND FIFTH IN 1969. IT WAS TIME FOR MANTLE TO THINK ABOUT THE FUTURE. HE RETIRED IN 1969. OVER SIXTY THOUSAND FANS SHOWED UP ON JUNE 8, 1969, TO SEE MANTLE'S NUMBER "7" OFFICIALLY RETIRED.

."The Voices of the Yankees" .

Mel Allen called the Yankee plays from 1939 to 1964, leading his listeners through the intricacies of the game. As a fluke, this native Alabaman had tried out for and won the job as announcer for CBS Radio. His soft southern voice was soothing to New Yorkers used to the grating accents of the Bronx and Brooklyn. Through the years, Allen is credited with naming many Yankee players: Joe DiMaggio was "Joltin' Joe," Phil Rizzuto was "Scooter," and Tommy Henrich was "Old Reliable." His slick reportage of a home run—"Going, going, gone!"—packed the drama into the moment of the hit, and remains in use today.

Phil Rizzuto was crushed when George Weiss cut him in 1956—but he was born again as a Yankee broadcaster alongside Mel Allen and Red Barber. He stayed on the air for thirty-nine years—with his high-pitched, excitable, Brooklynite voice rising to a crescendo with his favorite expression, "Hooooooooly Cow!"

ROGER MARIS

Yr.	Team	G	BA	SA	AB	H	2B	3B	HR	R	RBI	BB	SB
1957	CLE A	116	.235	.405	358	84	9	5	14	61	51	60	8
1958	2 teams	CLE A (51G - .225)			KC A (99G - .247)								
"	total	150	.240	.431	583	140	19	4	28	87	80	45	4
1959	KC A	122	.273	.464	433	118	21	7	16	69	72	58	2
1960	NY A	136	.283	.581	499	141	18	7	39	98	112	70	2
1961		161	.269	.620	590	159	16	4	61	132	142	94	0
1962		157	.256	.485	590	151	34	1	33	92	100	87	1
1963		90	.269	.542	312	84	14	1	23	53	53	35	1
1964		141	.281	.464	513	144	12	2	26	86	71	62	3
1965		46	.239	.439	155	37	7	0	8	22	27	29	0
1966		119	.233	.382	348	81	9	2	13	37	43	36	0
1967	STL N	125	.261	.405	410	107	18	7	9	64	55	52	0
1968		100	.255	.374	310	79	18	2	5	25	45	24	0
12 yrs.		1463	.260	.476	5101	1325	195	42	275	826	851	652	21
WORLD SERIES													
1960	NY A	7	.267	.500	30	8	1	0	2	6	2	2	0
1961		5	.105	.316	19	2	1	0	1	4	2	4	0
1962		7	.174	.348	23	4	1	0	1	4	5	5	0
1963		2	.000	.000	5	0	0	0	0	0	0	0	0
1964		7	.200	.300	30	6	0	0	1	4	1	1	0
1967	STL N	7	.385	.538	26	10	1	0	1	3	7	3	0
1968		6	.158	.211	19	3	1	0	0	5	1	3	0
7 yrs.		41	.217	.368	152	33	5	0	6	26	18	18	0
		10th			10th						6th		

GEORGE STEINBRENNER BOUGHT THE YANKS IN 1973. GLOBE PHOTOS, INC.

The *Seventies* and *Eighties*

WITH RALPH HOUK BACK IN PLACE, THE YANKEES BEGAN THE 1970S without a look back. In 1970, they finished a surprising second in the AL East (the Leagues expanded in 1969, adding two more to the AL). They were so-so in 1971, managed to earn second again in 1972, and dropped back to fourth in

1973. Attendance at the stadium remained dismal—New Yorkers were no longer flocking to the aging ball-park. Afer the 1973 season, the Yanks moved to Shea Stadium while the old ballpark received a major face-lift. But the Yankees need more than cosmetic changes.

Mickey Mantle, Yogi Berra, and Whitey Ford were gone. Phil Rizzuto was gone, off the field and into the broadcasting booth. Everything seemed out of whack. CBS was becoming disenchanted with its pur-chase of the Yankees, and wanted out of baseball generally.

The Yankees needed a leader. And George Stein-brenner, a businessman who wanted to win baseball games above all else, and win them with the Yankees, seemed like just the man.

CBS had given Mike Burke the orders: Unload the team for the most money you can get—but do it fast.

On June 3, 1973, the papers were signed. George Steinbrenner (or actually a group of men headed by Steinbrenner) bought the New York Yankees for $10 million. And Steinbrenner had more money, plenty of it. Money he was willing to spend to turn the team around.

It was the first year of free agency—players were able to negotiate their own contracts and move from team to team. Steinbrenner used this freedom to ac-quire major stars.

Boss George wanted glamour in his team—not just good players. And glamour was what he paid big bucks for. He got Jim Hunter, a pitcher nicknamed "Catfish," for $3.35 million in 1975. He got an up-and-coming big league slugger named Reggie Jackson for $2.66 million in 1977. And he got Goose Gossage, a top reliever, for $2.75 million in 1978. He fired his top execs and sold or traded half of the team for new stars like Lou Piniella, Graig Nettles, and Chris Chambliss.

The stadium was refurbished, the new players came through, manager Billy Martin was doing a bang-up job—by George, it seemed to have worked. The Yankees won the pennant and made it to the World Series in 1976, for the first time in twelve years. Fans came to watch in droves, even forgiving the team for ultimately losing the Series to the Cincinnati Reds.

Steinbrenner's involved style plus impetuous decision making reminded the public of the old days when Jacob Ruppert had purchased the Yankees and began making changes in his own inimitable fashion. The press dubbed Steinbrenner "Boss" and the stories coming out were focused on Boss George rather than on the team. The writers lined up on either side of an invisible line: for him or against him.

He became an instant controversy, a constant source of material for writers, and a publicity machine. His picture frequently appeared in the paper and he was a guest on radio talk shows all the time.

Would he bring the Yankees back? It all depended on the group he'd paid good money for: Reggie Jackson, Billy Martin (as manager), and Don Mattingly.

• "Boss George" •

George Steinbrenner's temper—and his tough take-it-or-leave-it approach—has made him something of a legend. He's been immortalized in the popular television series *Seinfeld* (the character Steinbrenner is never seen on-camera; his intolerance for mistakes is heard in his loud, barking voice). New Yorkers blamed Steinbrenner for the disappointing 1981 Series—Reggie Jackson left the team furious with Steinbrenner. Complications stemming from his 1980s debacle with free-agent Dave Winfield resulted in his resignation as Managing General Partner in 1990. He returned in 1993, as controversial a figure as ever. The Series win in 1996 certainly helped his reputation.

Reggie Jackson was the perfect image maker for the Yankees. Steinbrenner signed him in 1977, impressed by Jackson's excellent track record.

In 1969, he hit 47 home runs with the Athletics, and led Oakland to 3 straight World Championships (1972–1974). In 1976 he was traded to Baltimore, where he hit 27 home runs with 91 RBIs. At the end of that season, he entered the first free agent reentry draft. Skirmishes with manager Billy Martin and others marred his first year with the Yanks, but in the end he hit 32 home runs, drove the Yanks to a division title and led the club in RBIs (110), doubles (39), walks (75), and slugging (.550).

Game 6 of the 1977 World Series at Yankee Stadium established Reggie Jackson as a Yankees hero. He hit 3 home runs in a row, each one on a first pitch. The Yankees beat the Dodgers to win the team's first World Championship since 1962. After the third home run registered, the Stadium was shaking with cries of "Reggie! Reggie! Reggie!"

REGGIE JACKSON HELPED THE TEAM WIN THE WORLD SERIES IN 1977.
GLOBE PHOTOS, INC.

The feud festering between Martin and Jackson broke out into the open on July 17, 1978. Jackson attempted a sacrifice bunt against Martin's orders to hit away. He struck out and the Yanks lost, falling 14 games behind Boston. The punishment: Jackson was suspended for five days. Grousing to sportswriters, Martin said that Reggie Jackson and George Steinbrenner "deserved each other." The next day Martin was out as manager. Less than a week later, he was in again.

Despite this turmoil, Jackson had a good year in 1978, tied Graig Nettles for club leadership in home runs (27), and led the Yanks in RBIs (97), and slugging (.477). He hit a homer in the Yankees playoff win at Boston. Jackson's combined postseason stats were great. He hit .400 with 5 home runs and 15 RBIs in 11 games. Jackson's 2-run homer in Game 6 of the Series cinched the title.

1978 goes down as a winning year, with left-handed pitcher Ron Guidry earning honors all around and a pitching record (25–3) to be proud of. 1979 saw the death of star catcher Thurman Munson and the return of Billy Martin. Reggie Jackson led the 1979 Yanks in hitting (29 HR, 89 RBIs, .544 slugging), but the team failed to take a pennant. And Billy Martin

Q. One Yankee player once said this about another Yankee player: "He'd give you the shirt off his back. Of course, he'd call a press conference to announce it." Who said that about which other player?

Q. Who was the World Series MVP in 1977?

A. Reggie Jackson, who also won it four years earlier when he was with Oakland.

A. Catfish Hunter said it about Reggie Jackson.

was fired again, this time for lying to Steinbrenner about a fight he'd been in. Rookie Dick Howser replaced him.

1980 proved to be Jackson's best season. He hit a total of 41 home runs, the most by a Yankee since 1961. He led the Yankees in hits (154), RBIs (111, the most since Mantle's 111 in 1964), and slugging (.597, the highest since Mantle's .605 in 1962). He homered in his fourth consecutive game on October 4; the Yanks had the division title again.

Much to the fans' dismay, in 1981 Steinbrenner cut off contract negotiations with Jackson, after Jackson arrived late to spring training. A players strike occurred on June 12, and Jackson, his free agency just around the corner, was planning to leave the Yanks by the late season. Still, in Game 5 of the Division Series with Milwaukee, he slammed a 2-run homer, helping the Yankees to win. A calf injury combined with Steinbrenner's wrath (Jackson had picked a fight with Graig Nettles) resulted in Jackson sitting out the first 3 games of the 1981 World Series. In Game 4, he homered, hit 2 singles, and walked twice. Jackson also earned an error when he lost a fly ball in the sun. The Dodgers won the Series in Game 6, and Jackson was out of there.

The icing on the cake of the 1981 season: George Steinbrenner's abject apology to New York City for losing the World Series to the Brooklyn Dodgers. In fact, with Reggie Jackson gone for good, the future looked bleak.

1982 *was* grim (79–83; fifth place), but in 1983 Billy Martin came back, helping the team to a more respectable 91–71 record (third place). After yet another managerial switch, Yogi Berra managed

BILLY MARTIN. DAVID WOO/GLOBE PHOTOS, INC.

the mediocre 1984 team. Then Billy Martin was back.

Things looked good for 1985. Don Mattingly showed himself to be a team leader, and an amazing first baseman. The Yanks had Dave Winfield, a hard-hitting slugger from the San Diego Padres and Rickey Henderson, a base-stealing champion from the Oakland Athletics. Henderson led the American League in stolen bases (80) and made the club record in 1988 with 93 SBs. He was the most valuable leadoff man that the Yanks had ever seen.

Winfield was a standout too, helping the Yanks forget that Reggie Jackson was missing. He had five seasons with over 100 RBIs and hit 24 home runs in each of his full seasons, all the while battling ferociously with Boss George about his payout. In 1990 Steinbrenner traded him away to the California Angels. (The scandal forced legal action and Steinbrenner left the Yanks for a short period.)

From the mid-eighties on, Don Mattingly represented the essence of Yankeeism. He seemed to wear the invisible mantle of the "Yankee of the future," installed at first base as the fans' number one player for at least a decade.

Before the pros, Mattingly was considered a rather slow runner with a mediocre amount of batting power. He was drafted in 1979, and worked through the minors. In 1982, he was called up; 1984 was his first full season as a Yankee regular. Named team captain, he won the American League batting title in 1984, and

DON MATTINGLY SEEMED TO REPRESENT
"THE ESSENCE OF THE YANKEES."
GLOBE PHOTOS, INC.

in 1985 was voted Most Valuable Player in the American League.

Mattingly realized his shortcomings and worked on them diligently.

1984 to 1989 were undoubtedly Mattingly's best years. Unfortunately, however, he had developed a back problem that simply would not go away.

Still he kept on, coming close to a World Series Game in 1995. But that was the end. The back became too painful, so Mattingly passed up the 1996 season.

In his final six seasons, Mattingly had hit a total of 58 home runs and averaged 64 RBIs. A fitting companion for Ruth, Gehrig, DiMaggio, and Mantle.

• "When he was bad . . ." •

Billy Martin had a rocky career managing the Yanks—he was as likely to get beaten up as he was to earn good stats. The first time the scrappy former Yankee was hired by George Steinbrenner, he got the team 3 pennants. He was fired after calling Boss George and Reggie Jackson liars. Then he was back managing again. He punched an argumentative fan and was out again. He worked for Oakland for two years, then; got fired. He came back to New York and was hired and fired a few more times. He was a wild man as a player and as a manager. On Christmas Day, 1989, after a celebration in a bar near his home, Martin died in a car wreck.

DON MATTINGLY

Yr.	Team	G	BA	SA	AB	H	2B	3B	HR	R	RBI	BB	SB
1982	NY A	7	.167	.167	12	2	0	0	0	0	1	0	0
1983		91	.283	.409	279	79	15	4	4	34	32	21	0
1984		153	.343	.537	603	207	44	2	23	91	110	41	1
1985		159	.324	.567	652	211	48	3	35	107	145	56	2
1986		162	.352	.573	677	238	53	2	31	117	113	53	0
1987		141	.327	.559	569	186	38	2	30	93	115	51	1
1988		144	.311	.462	599	186	37	0	18	94	88	41	1
1989		158	.303	.477	631	191	37	2	23	79	113	51	3
1990		102	.256	.335	394	101	16	0	5	40	42	28	1
1991		152	.288	.394	587	169	35	0	9	64	68	46	2
1992		157	.287	.416	640	184	40	0	14	89	86	39	3
1993		134	.291	.445	530	154	27	2	17	78	86	61	0
1994		97	.304	.411	372	113	20	1	6	62	51	60	0
1995		128	.288	.413	458	132	32	2	7	59	49	40	0
14 yrs.		1785	.307	.471	7003	2153	442	20	222	1007	1099	588	14

REGGIE JACKSON

Yr.	Team	G	BA	SA	AB	H	2B	3B	HR	R	RBI	BB	SB
1967	KC A	35	.178	.305	118	21	4	4	1	13	6	10	1
1968	OAK A	154	.250	.452	553	138	13	6	29	82	74	50	14
1969		152	.275	.608	549	151	36	3	47	123	118	114	13
1970		149	.237	.458	426	101	21	2	23	57	66	75	26
1971		150	.277	.508	567	157	29	3	32	87	80	63	16
1972		135	.265	.473	499	132	25	2	25	72	75	59	9
1973		151	.293	.531	539	158	28	2	32	99	117	76	22
1974		148	.289	.514	506	146	25	1	29	90	93	86	25
1975		157	.253	.511	593	150	39	3	36	91	104	67	17
1976	BAL A	134	.277	.502	498	138	27	2	27	84	91	54	28
1977	NY A	146	.286	.550	525	150	39	2	32	93	110	74	17
1978		139	.274	.477	511	140	13	5	27	82	97	58	14
1979		131	.297	.544	465	138	24	2	29	78	89	65	9
1980		143	.300	.597	514	154	22	4	41	94	111	83	1
1981		94	.237	.428	334	79	17	1	15	33	54	46	0
1982	CAL A	153	.275	.532	530	146	17	1	39	92	101	85	4
1983		116	.194	.340	397	77	14	1	14	43	49	52	0
1984		143	.223	.406	525	117	17	2	25	67	81	55	8
1985		143	.252	.487	460	116	27	0	27	64	85	78	1
1986		132	.241	.408	419	101	12	2	18	65	58	92	1
1987	OAK A	115	.220	.402	336	74	14	1	15	42	43	33	2
21 yrs.		2820	.262	.490	9864	2584	463	49	563 6th	1551	1702	1375	228

DIVISIONAL PLAYOFF SERIES

Yr.	Team	G	BA	SA	AB	H	2B	3B	HR	R	RBI	BB	SB
1981	NY A	5	.300	.600	20	6	0	0	2	4	4	1	0

REGGIE JACKSON (CON'T)

Yr.	Team	G	BA	SA	AB	H	2B	3B	HR	R	RBI	BB	SB
LEAGUE CHAMPIONSHIP SERIES													
1971	OAK A	3	.333	.917	12	4	1	0	2	2	2	0	0
1972		5	.278	.333	18	5	1	0	0	1	2	1	2
1973		5	.143	.143	21	3	0	0	0	0	0	0	0
1974		4	.167	.250	12	2	1	0	0	0	1	5	0
1975		3	.417	.667	12	5	0	0	1	1	3	0	0
1977	NY A	5	.125	.125	16	2	0	0	0	1	1	2	1
1978		4	.462	1.000	13	6	1	0	2	5	6	3	0
1980		3	.273	.364	11	3	1	0	0	1	0	1	0
1981		2	.000	.000	4	0	0	0	0	1	1	1	1
1982	CAL A	5	.111	.278	18	2	0	0	1	2	2	2	0
1986		6	.192	.269	26	5	2	0	0	2	2	2	0
11 yrs.		45	.227	.380	163	37	7	0	6	16	20	17	4
		1st			1st	2nd	1st		3rd	4th	2nd	2nd	
WORLD SERIES													
1973	OAK A	7	.310	.586	29	9	3	1	1	3	6	2	0
1974		5	.286	.571	14	4	1	0	1	3	1	5	1
1977	NY A	6	.450	1.250	20	9	1	0	5	10	8	3	0
1978		6	.391	.696	23	9	1	0	2	2	8	3	0
1981		3	.333	.667	12	4	1	0	1	3	1	2	0
5 yrs.		27	.357	.755	98	35	7	1	10	21	24	15	1
				1st					5th	10th	8th		

The
Nineties

IN THE YEAR THAT OPENED UP THE
DECADE OF THE 1990S THE YANKEES
hit rock bottom—last in the American
League. If the Yanks could rally, there
was no place to go but up. It
wouldn't be easy. Steinbrenner was
suspended from baseball (originally for life; this
was reduced to 30 months) after an investigation

into his connections with a New York gambler. The new manager, Stump Merrill, was a tobacco-chewing minor league old-timer from the glory days of baseball, old-fashioned in a way that the team members certainly were not.

Don Mattingly kept the team together. (Merrill was *not* a hit!) As captain, he helped prevent the Yankees from dropping into the absolute pits during the early nineties.

The sun shone through, when stars-to-be were acquired, or more veteran team members came into their own. The brightest of this bunch, Bernie Williams, signed on in 1985 when he was only seventeen years old, and waited six years to actually play with the Yankees. In 1991 Williams took over center field. But it was his switch-hit batting that would make him a superstar. In and out of the minors during his first years, Williams hit 12 home runs in 1993, with 68 RBIs, and a 21-game hitting streak.

In 1994, he played 108 games until the players strike, hitting 29 doubles, 12 homers, 57 RBIs, 80

runs, 61 walks, and 16 stolen bases. In 1995 he finished with a .307 batting average with 93 runs and
82 RBIs. In the playoffs he batted .429 (9 for 21).

Not only did Williams score, he was the most po-
lite player on the team.

New Yorkers—a gruff, brash breed—couldn't figure Williams out. They wondered about an athlete
who played classic guitar on a Fender Stratocaster.
Was he a musician or a ballplayer?

BERNIE WILLIAMS. AP PHOTO/DAVID MARTIN

107

• "Hitting the Right Notes" •

Bernie Williams came up from La Escuela Libre de Musica in Puerto Rico, where he excelled at classic guitar and piano. He signed on with the Yankees at the age of seventeen for sixteen grand a year.

It was a long road to success for Bernie Williams. Baltimore hitting coach Rick Down, who had coached for New York too, said of him: "No one should have to use the word 'potential' again with Bernie. He's done it. He used to let his first two at-bats affect his last two at-bats. Not anymore. He's in control. Nothing flusters him now. He used to get off to slow starts, have bad Aprils or whatever. Now I think you'll see a consistent player in control from Day One of the season."

Despite the accolades from those who played with him and against him, Williams remains the prototype of modesty.

"I never take this job for granted," he told a reporter. "I never lose sight of the ones who have come before me out there. It's not just Mr. DiMaggio and Mickey Mantle. You think about Bobby Murcer and Mickey Rivers. You think about the kind of center field Paul Blair played when he was a Yankee. The truth is, the best thing for me is to not think about those people too much. The best thing for me is to keep going."

There was more. "People keep telling me that I've changed or stepped it up or things like that. I don't really think so. I've grown, like anyone else. I've adjusted. But I'm the same person."

Every rookie grapples with the changes success brings. 1995 rookie pitcher Andy Pettitte had to learn that perfectionism can sometimes leave one crying. When he was only six years old, he wept unconsolably the day after his football team lost a game to their opposition. It wasn't just the loss.

Tom Pettitte, his father, remembered how Andy said he was crying because the team lost and the other kids didn't seem to care.

By 1995, Pettitte had learned to control the tears, but he continued to strive for perfection: "I've been that way since Little League. Whatever I do, I love to win. I love the competition. I don't care if it's tennis or Ping-Pong. Whatever it is, I'll kill myself to win it."

Born in Louisiana, Pettitte had moved to Texas by fourth grade, and spent much of his childhood playing baseball.

Pettitte was signed on by the Yankees as a free agent in 1991, from San Jacinto Junior College in Texas. The next years were tough ones, during which he had to climb his way up the minor league ladder. But he finally made it, and was signed on with the Yankees in 1995 as a rookie pitcher.

He impressed Joe Girardi, the Yankee catcher, with his consistency in pitching: "There's only been one or two starts that he hasn't had his good stuff. He's usually pretty consistent with what he brings to the game. That's what makes him so good."

Pettitte worked hard, experimenting with different kinds of throws. By the time he had gotten into professional baseball, he had developed into a control pitcher who could mix speeds that would keep the batters off balance. He had an arsenal of pitches: the fastball, the change-up, the curveball, and the cut-fastball.

Catcher Girardi: "What makes him so great is that he can use four pitches at any time. I don't think he has one pitch that stands out at maybe being the best

ANDY PETTITE JOINED THE YANKS IN 1995 AS A ROOKIE PITCHER.
AP PHOTO/JOHN BAZEMORE

one in baseball. You know—best fastball, best curve. He's got great command."

Suddenly Pettitte developed another good secret weapon. He became one of the best pick-off men in the American League. During his rookie year he caught twelve runners in all. Not bad for a rookie!

Reporters griped about Pettitte constantly, saying he never said anything good to quote. "I'm pretty boring," Pettitte once admitted.

A BRIGHT SPOT IN THE EARLY 1990S,
JIMMY KEY'S MOST FAMOUS GAMES WERE TO COME.
GLOBE PHOTOS, INC. PHOTOS, INC.

His father summed it up. "What you see with Andy is the way he's been all his life. He's low-key and he doesn't try to impress people. He just wants to pitch."

There were other bright spots in the Yankee lineup in the early 1990s—particularly with Derek Jeter, Wade Boggs, and Jimmy Key—but Bernie Williams and Andy Pettitte stand out brightly. And a time was rapidly approaching when they would be tested to the utmost in the crucible of major league play-offs—and the battle for the World Championship in Baseball.

NEW YORK YANKEES' JIM LEYRITZ (13) IS MOBBED BY TEAMMATES AFTER HIS EIGHTH-INNING
3-RUN HOME RUN IN GAME 4 OF THE WORLD SERIES. AP PHOTO/PAT SULLIVAN

The Championship Year:
1996

AT 11:56 ON THE NIGHT OF GAME 6 OF THE SERIES THE STANDS IN Yankee Stadium went wild. The players and every Yankee fan everywhere went wild. The Bronx Bombers had taken their twenty-third World Series—the first in eighteen years—beating the title-holding Braves. There wasn't a Murderers'

Row; there was no Bambino. It was all about being a team.

From spring training on, the Yanks worked at playing well together and built up steady solid momentum— and stats. And there was the good news. Bright young shortstop Derek Jeter started Opening Day against Cleveland off right with a homer—the first of his career in the majors. On May 14, Doc Gooden threw his no-hitter against the Mariners. The Yankees were in first place in the American League in July. And rookie pitcher Andy Pettitte was 12 and 2 at the end of August. Also by then there was a pretty impressive

DEREK JETER. GLOBE PHOTOS, INC.

list of new blood—Darryl Strawberry, Cecil Fielder, David Weathers, Graeme Lloyd, and Charlie Hayes who was returning to the fold.

• "Jeter's Amazing Stats" •

Derek Jeter's eighth-grade yearbook predicted that Jeter would be a Yankee one day . . . and he turned out to be not just *any* Yankee. In 1996, Jeter won the 1996 American League Rookie of the Year, with truly amazing stats: In 157 games, he was at bat 583 times, and had 183 hits with 104 runs, including 25 doubles and 6 triples. He threw in 10 home runs for good measure. He walked 48 times, stole 14 bases, batted in 78 runs, and had a batting average in 1996 of .314. He was serious about being a strictly work-ethic guy. "I don't worry about what others say about my play or what others think. On the field, I'll just go out there, do the best that I can, and try to play baseball the way I should. I play hard."

On the flip side—besides no Mattingly—an aneurysm in the right shoulder of their number one starter, David Cone, took him out of the rotation in May—nobody knew for how long.

But the Yanks kept going, stacking up the stats,

looking at some postseason play. Then on September 2, Cone was back, the leadoff in a road game against Oakland—and for 7 innings held the Athletics hitless. Three weeks later, needing only 1 win over the Brewers for the AL East Division title, with Cone on the mound, the Yankees got it with overkill, taking the title, 19–2.

• "Magic Trick" •

Game 1 of the playoffs between the New York Yankees and the Baltimore Orioles: In the eighth inning Derek Jeter, batting against Armando Benitez of the Orioles, hit a fly ball to deep right. Tony Tarasco ran to the fence to field it—but the ball never came down. "It was like a magic trick," he said later. "I was camped underneath the ball. If the ball was going out, I would've at least tried to jump. It was magic." TV replays showed a boy had intercepted the fly ball with his baseball glove, which he stuck out over the wall to catch the ball. Umpire Rich Garcia ruled the ball a home run; to him, it had gone over the wall and into the stands. Even Jeff Maier, the twelve-year-old kid who reached out for the ball, said, "I really didn't know whether it went over the wall or not." Viewing the tapes later, Garcia admitted he had erred. Tied at 4–4, the game went into the eleventh when Bernie Williams lofted a high one into the stands for the game-winning home run. Maier was lionized by the New York media, appeared on TV, and went home a star. The Orioles were not as thrilled . . .

After dusting Texas and Baltimore in October, the Bronx Bombers went for big-time postseason play. The Series, like the season, was all about the team. The first team to win 4 straight after losing their first 2 at home. For a bad start, New York was resting while Atlanta was finishing the playoffs, and Opening Day October 19 was rained out. Then Andy Pettitte openhandedly gave Game 1 to Smoltz. Said Wade Boggs, "We ran into a buzz saw." In Game 2, Maddox shut out New York—in 8 innings only 20 of his 82 pitches were balls—"It turned out that Maddux's mastery so bored the stadium faithful that many of them took to running onto the field for entertainment. By the ninth inning, twice as many fans had reached second base (four) as Yankees (two)." More generous-minded Yankee fans might own that those two games were a chance to watch some beautiful pitching.

In Atlanta, on *their* turf, Cone turned the whole thing around in the bottom of the sixth with his 2–0 lead, the bases loaded, and 1 out. (Two more outs and New York would have trailed 3 games.) When Torre trotted out to the mound, Cone smooth-talked him into staying, saying although he was losing his splitter his fastball was okay. (Okay. His fastballs went as high as 93 mph—2 mph over his usual tops.) Then in the

DAVID CONE COMES THROUGH IN GAME 3 OF THE SERIES.

GLOBE PHOTOS, INC.

next inning Bernie Williams whacked a 2-run homer. The next day Joe Torre said that the sixth inning was the whole Series to him.

In Game 4 starter Kenny Rogers wasn't brilliant—in the sixth the Yanks still trailed. Jim Leyritz with a 3-run homer in the eighth for a tie started the turning tide. And Wetteland posted the winning numbers in the tenth, 8–6 Yanks.

"I NEVER THOUGHT I WAS GOING TO GET HERE. I WAS FIRED LAST YEAR AND I THOUGHT THAT WAS MY LAST STOP. IT'S VERY EMOTIONAL TO FINALLY GET HERE. . . . I WISH THIS FEELING COULD LAST FOREVER." —JOE TORRE, AFTER WINNING THE 1996 SERIES

The home run Bernie Williams hit in the eighth inning of Game 3 of the World Series in 1996 was his sixth home run since the beginning of the playoffs, which tied a record set by Bob Robertson of Pittsburgh in 1971 and matched by Len Dykstra in 1993 and Ken Griffey, Jr., in 1995.

In Game 5, Pettitte and Smoltz faced off again, giving Andy another chance. It was Andy's game—for 8⅓ innings swinging the Series in the Yankees' favor. The Bombers shut out the Braves, 1–0, with Charlie Hayes, on second because Grissom had dropped his **121** fly ball, scoring later on a double by Fielder. Wetteland stepped in in the ninth, for his second night, to sew up Pettitte's victory. And Paul O'Neill, his hamstring strained and hurting, in the top of the ninth with one on in scoring position, chased down Luis Polonia's line drive into deep right center for the game-saving catch. O'Neill's comment: "Later on, Tino Martinez told me, 'You know, if you don't catch that ball, we lose the game.' "

• "Strawberry is *back*." •

The clout that Darryl Strawberry administered to the baseball during the third inning of Game 5 of the American League Championship Series was not one of those "just barely" home runs that might have been expected from a man who had been a superstar for the New York Mets but was now no more than a comeback kid for the New York Yankees. No. It was a full-fledged home run of 448 feet—the kind of big slam that had the tape measures out counting when Mickey Mantle first came to town. With Strawberry, it meant he was back—*really* back. After struggling with drug and alcohol abuse, he had signed with the Yankees July 4, 1996. During the 1996 season with the Yankees he batted .262 with 11 homers in 63 regular-season games. The smash against the Orioles in Game 5 of the ALCS was icing on the cake. For the series he batted .417, hit 3 homers, and set a League Championship Series record with a 1.167 slugging percentage. Not bad at all for a "has-been"!

The last game was Key and Maddux. Maddux was tough to break until the third. O'Neill hit him, then Girardi—who'd formerly caught him with the Cubs—got himself to third and was sent home on a single by Jeter. Atlanta got 2 runs after that but, in the bottom of the ninth, was denied a third. Mark Lemke's second pop-

DARRYL STRAWBERRY. GLOBE PHOTOS, INC.

per off a fastball from Wetteland (his third night in a row) was retrieved by Charlie Hayes all-smiles by the Atlanta dugout. The fat lady was singing.

• "An Emotional Win" •

It would have made a boffo Hollywood scenario. "I was the baby of the family," Joe Torre once said. "I had a lot of parents. I was supposed to be a doctor. Then a priest. I took a little of each and played baseball."

None too successfully. Up to 1996 he had played and/or managed 4,722 games without ever getting near a

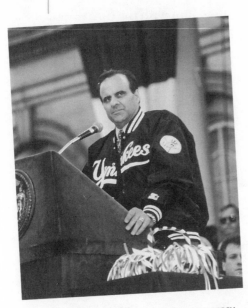

JOE TORRE REFLECTS ON THE YANKEES' SUCCESS STORY.
WALTER WEISSMAN/GLOBE PHOTOS, INC.

World Series and then in June 1995 he was fired as the St. Louis manager for a career-ending blow. But five months later the Yankees hired him. Unfortunately, Torre's personal life took a sad turn when his brother Rocco died in June 1996. Then, two months later, his formerly baseball-playing brother Frank waited eleven critical weeks for a heart transplant. Joe used Frank as a co-manager of the Yankees during this time, receiving advice and tips by telephone as Frank awaited news of a heart donor. Then, on the day before the last game of the World Series against the Atlanta Braves, Frank got a new heart. And on the very next day, Joe won the biggest game of his career, becoming the winning World Series manager. Who in real life could star in such a Hollywood extravaganza as that—and make it look real?

NEW YORK YANKEES CHAMPIONSHIP SEASONS—MORE THAN ANY OTHER TEAM IN BASEBALL HISTORY:

Year	Opponent	Series Games
1923	New York	4–2
1927	Pittsburgh	4–0
1928	St. Louis	4–0
1932	Chicago Cubs	4–0
1936	New York	4–2
1937	New York	4–1
1938	Chicago Cubs	4–0
1939	Cincinnati	4–0
1941	Brooklyn	4–1
1943	St. Louis	4–1
1947	Brooklyn	4–3
1949	Brooklyn	4–1
1950	Philadelphia	4–0
1951	New York	4–2
1952	Brooklyn	4–3
1953	Brooklyn	4–2
1956	Brooklyn	4–3
1958	Milwaukee	4–3
1961	Cincinnati	4–1
1962	San Francisco	4–3
1977	Los Angeles	4–2
1978	Los Angeles	4–2
1996	Atlanta	4–2

The New York Yankees have more members enshrined in the Baseball Hall of Fame than any other team—30 to be exact. Here they are:

YANKEE HALL OF FAMERS

1936	Babe Ruth
1939	Willie Keeler
1939	Lou Gehrig
1946	Frank Chance
1946	Jack Chesbro
1948	Herb Pennock
1954	Bill Dickey
1955	Joe DiMaggio
1955	Frank Baker
1957	Joe McCarthy
1964	Miller Huggins
1966	Casey Stengel
1967	Red Ruffing
1969	Waite Hoyt
1970	Earle Combs
1972	Yogi Berra
1972	Lefty Gomez
1974	Mickey Mantle
1974	Whitey Ford
1976	Bob Lemon
1977	Joe Sewell
1981	Johnny Mize
1985	Enos Slaughter
1987	Catfish Hunter
1991	Tony Lazzero
1993	Reggie Jackson
1994	Phil Rizzuto
(and these executives)	
1953	Ed Barrow
1971	George Weiss
1978	Larry MacPhail

· The Yankees Have the Most American League MVPS in History ·

Three time winners:
  Joe DiMaggio ('39, '41, '47)
  Yogi Berra ('51, '54, '55)
  Mickey Mantle ('56, '57, '62)

Two-time winners:
  Lou Gehrig ('27, '36)
  Roger Maris ('60, '61)

One-time winners:
  Babe Ruth ('23)
  Joe Gordon ('42)
  Spud Chandler ('43)
  Phil Rizzuto ('50)
  Elston Howard ('63)
  Thurman Munson ('76)
  Don Mattingly ('85)